BROWNIES,
BARS & GOODIES
GALORE

BROWNIES, BARS & GOODIES
GALORE

JO McAULEY

spruce

An Hachette UK Company

First published in Great Britain in 2010
by Spruce, a division of
Octopus Publishing Group Ltd
Endeavour House, 189 Shaftesbury Avenue,
London, WC2H 8JY
www.octopusbooks.co.uk
www.octopusbooksusa.com

Distributed in the U.S.A. and Canada for
Octopus Books USA
c/- Hachette Book Group USA
237 Park Avenue
New York, NY 10017

Photography: Ian Garlick
Food Styling: Eliza Baird
Page Layout: Phil Gilderdale

ISBN 13 978-1-84601-373-7
ISBN 10 1-84601-373-9

Printed and bound in China

10 9 8 7 6 5 4 3 2 1

This book includes dishes made with nuts and
nut derivatives. It is advisable for those with
known allergic reactions to nuts and nut
derivatives and those who may be potentially
vulnerable to these allergies, such as pregnant
and nursing mothers, invalids, the elderly,
babies, and children, to avoid dishes make
with nuts and nut oils. It is also prudent to
check the labels of prepared ingredients for
the possible inclusion of nut derivatives.

Ovens should be preheated to the specific
temperature. If using a fan-assisted oven,
follow the manufacturer's instructions for
adjusting the time and temperature.

CONTENTS

INTRODUCTION

Wonderful smells, warmth, and satisfaction are just some of the things that a home-baked cake can bring. The range, simplicity, and outstanding results of the recipes in this book will leave you wondering why it has taken you so long to make your own homemade cakes!

★ VERSATILE TREATS ★

Whether you need a recipe for an impressive cake to celebrate a special occasion, or a big batch of sheet cakes to help out a school cake sale, you will find what you're looking for here. Not only is it often less expensive to make your own cake than buying one from a supermarket, but the quality is infinitely better. With no unpleasant artificial flavorings or preservatives, you know exactly what's going into your cake.

★ BROWNIES ★

These treats are increasingly popular due to their ease and versatility. It is possible to whip up a batch of incredible-tasting brownies, or their golden equivalent "blondies," in practically no time, and often you don't even need to wait for them to cool properly because they can usually be eaten still warm from the oven. Served as they are or with a drizzle, frosting, or a scoop of ice cream, there is a brownie recipe here to please everyone!

★ SHEET CAKES & BARS ★

Sheet cakes are usually cakes that are simple to make, cooked in a deep baking sheet or pan and cut up into squares. They are perfect for afternoon snacks, a cake sale event, or as a delicious dessert to finish any meal. Most are easy to freeze, although this is best done before the frosting stage.

Bars are also a type of sheet cake, easily cut into slices, squares, fingers, or bars. However, they are less "cakey" and usually have a cookie or pastry base, or else are a kind of oaty, cereal bar. They are easy to transport and package, making them a great choice to take to a party, school, or picnic, or just to cut up to serve as an after-school or work snack.

★ OTHER SMALL BAKED GOODIES ★

Other chapters in this book cover smaller bakes, such as muffins, which are ideal for a homemade breakfast, a leisurely brunch, or just as a satisfying afternoon snack. Pretty little cupcakes can also be found here, just waiting to be baked as a treat for kids and grown-ups alike—and you can even get everyone in the kitchen together to mix and decorate the finished cakes. Much more delicate than muffins, they would be perfect for an afternoon social gathering or arranged on a high plate as a novel dessert.

You can also have a try at baking delicate French Madeleines, Greek Ravanie, or Australian Lamingtons. So whether you fancy making a classic chocolate brownie, or a baklava-inspired pastry tart, something to share or something to store, you will find what you are looking for in this book, full of recipes that guarantee a kitchen full of delicious, home-baked aromas galore!

INGREDIENTS

The quality of the ingredients you bake with is important, because they can affect the final result in both appearance and taste. We recommend that you always buy the best-quality ingredients that you can find. Below are some notes on important or more unusual ingredients.

★ FLOUR ★

Because flours can vary and alter the end result of any cake, use a brand you know and are comfortable working with. All-purpose flour has no rising agents added, so a recipe will often call for you to add just the right amount in the correct form. Some recipes call for self-rising flour, which has rising agents already added to it. If you do not have self-rising flour at hand, you can substitute 1 cup all-purpose flour, 1½ teaspoons baking powder, and ⅛ teaspoon salt for each 1 cup self-rising flour. Whole-wheat flour is made using the whole wheat grain and is ground along with the bran and wheat grain.

★ RISING AGENTS ★

The rising agents used in this book, other than self-rising flour, which already has some rising agent added, are baking powder, baking soda, and cream of tartar.

★ SUGAR ★

More often than not, the sweetness in cakes comes from added sugar. This could be superfine or granulated sugar, light or dark brown sugar, or crunchy turbinado sugar (a raw brown sugar). Some recipes will call for a liquid sweetness in the form of honey, corn syrup (golden syrup), or maple syrup.

★ BUTTER ★

The butter used in these recipes is sweet (unsalted) and at room temperature unless otherwise stated. Butter produces a better flavor in baking, but can be substituted with margarine in most circumstances.

★ EGGS ★

Always keep eggs at an ambient temperature when using them in baking because it helps to prevent them from curdling. Use extra-large eggs unless otherwise stated and free-range and organic whenever possible. This not only ensures they have come from a "happy" hen, but will also improve the taste of your baking.

★ CHOCOLATE ★

Always buy good-quality chocolate for cooking with. Not only will it affect the end taste if you buy lower-quality and cocoa content chocolate, but it will also be harder to work with. Buy dark chocolate with a minimum 70 percent cocoa content and the best milk and white chocolate you can find.

★ FRUIT ★

Fresh and dried fruits are also used to bring sweet moistness to a cake in a way that sugar doesn't. Buy dried fruit that is semidried and still soft, not in its hard, dry, dehydrated form, unless otherwise stated. Fresh fruit can often be substituted with frozen.

★ CORNMEAL ★

Made from ground maize, cornmeal is popular in the South as grits and is known by Italians as polenta. If your meal comes with a mushy side dish of polenta in an Italian restaurant, you will be eating grits (Italians also bake polenta until firm). Cornmeal is widely available from supermarkets.

★ SPICES ★

Sweet spices, such as cinnamon, nutmeg, cloves, allspice, and ginger, are used to flavor some of the cakes and can be bought ground or in their whole form. To grind them yourself, you will need a spice grinder, cleaned between each use to avoid contaminating the flavors.

★ QUINOA ★

Puffed quinoa comes both unflavored and honey-coated and can be found in any good health food store.

★ LINSEEDS ★

Also known as flax, linseeds are small seeds that are a great form of omega-3 and can be bought at a health food store.

★ PUMPKIN SEEDS ★

Also known as pepitas, pumpkin seeds are used in this book in their raw, green, hulled condition. They are rich in protein as well as being a great source of iron, zinc, essential fatty acids, and magnesium.

★ EXTRACTS ★

Concentrated extracts are also used as flavoring in baking. Always use a natural choice whenever possible, such as natural vanilla extract.

TIPS FOR BAKING INGREDIENTS

★ Whatever the ingredient called for, it is important to use accurate amounts and measure correctly. The balance of ingredients, whether they are fats, flours, rising agents, or flavorings, have been carefully calculated for each recipe, so it is important to follow the recommendations given. There are a number of muffin recipes that you can simply double—it is indicated when recipes are suited to this.

★ Make sure that all ingredients are at room temperature before you begin baking, unless otherwise stated. Butter should be soft, for example, and eggs should not be used straight from the refrigerator.

★ Always follow the method to incorporate the ingredients in the order they are presented. It is important, for example, to avoid over-mixing muffins if you want the best results.

★ Brownies become firm as they cool, so don't be tempted to bake them for longer than suggested because they seem undercooked.

★ When using more than one shelf at the time when baking, space the oven shelves evenly to allow the air to circulate.

★ Most brownies, blondies, and sheet cakes will successfully freeze. Remember to always ensure they are completely cold first, and wrap them tightly in either plastic wrap or a plastic bag. If the bakes are already sliced, place parchment paper between layers.

EQUIPMENT

Having the right equipment is essential for the best results in baking, however, you don't need to buy everything at once. Invest in the basic essentials, buying the best quality that you can, and build upon these, adding an item or two at a time as needed.

★ MEASURING EQUIPMENT ★

Accurate measuring is important. You'll need a nested set of measuring cups—¼, ⅓, ½, and 1 cup are typical sizes—for dry ingredients. Unless otherwise stated, make sure the ingredients are level, using the back of a knife's blade to remove any excess. If you are measuring brown sugar, pack it into the cup before leveling it. Unless a preparation instruction is given after the ingredient, always prepare the ingredient before measuring. So, if the recipe says to use "1 cup sifted confectioners' sugar," sift the sugar before measuring. However, if it asks for "1 cup confectioners' sugar, sifted," make sure you measure the sugar before you sift it. If you fail to follow these instructions in the right order, you'll be using incorrect quantities, and the final result might be disappointing.

A liquid measuring cup should be glass or clear plastic so that you can easily see the level that the liquid comes to. When measuring, bend down so that the markings will be at your eye level.

You'll also need a set of standard kitchen measuring spoons for small amounts of both wet and dry ingredients. Do not be tempted to use spoons from your kitchen drawer, because these are simply not accurate enough for measuring.

★ BOWLS ★

A range of bowls and dishes in different sizes for measuring ingredients is useful, and it is important to have at least two large bowls for mixing because their size will help incorporate more air. However, this is not an issue when making brownies because you do not want to incorporate any extra air.

★ UTENSILS ★

A metal spatula is useful for loosening the edges of brownies and sheet cakes and lifting slices out of their baking sheets. A rubber, flexible spatula is best for scraping bowls clean and leveling surfaces of cake batter. You will also need wooden spoons for mixing, a large, metal spoon for folding effectively, and a chopping board and knife for those recipes that include nuts.

★ ELECTRIC BEATER ★

It saves a lot of time having at least a simple portable electric beater, especially because some recipes call for 10 minutes of beating with one.

★ PANS ★

There are so many different types of pans and baking sheets on the market. It is worth investing in good, nonstick baking sheets for brownies and sheet cakes. They need to be solid and strong. Thin, poorer-quality pans are more likely to warp and loose their shape over time. You can now buy a huge range of silicone bakeware that is particularly good for muffins and madeleines, thanks to its long life and nonstick properties. It is important to use the size of pans specified in the recipes, or as close as possible.

★ SIEVE ★

Most recipes do not require you to sift the flour, but for those that do you will need a fine stainless steel or plastic sieve.

★ PARCHMENT PAPER ★

You will save yourself a lot of hassle and have prettier cakes by using parchment paper to line your pans, even the nonstick types. When lining a pan it is a good idea to extend the parchment paper about 1 inch above the edges of the pan, as this will help when removing items from the pan.

★ TIMER ★

If you don't have a built-in timer on your oven, a little battery-operated one is worth purchasing.

★ OVEN MITTS ★

Reduce the risk of burns with a set of thick, heat resistant oven mitts.

★ COOLING RACKS ★

It is important to use cooling racks for cooling when recommended, to avoid baked items such as those with a cookie or pastry base going soggy. You can buy racks that fold away, making storage easy.

★ CONTAINERS ★

Invest in some airtight containers of different sizes to store all your delicious goodies and keep them fresh for another day.

THE ESSENTIAL OVEN

One of the most important aspects of home baking is a good oven with stable temperatures. If you have any doubts about your oven's accuracy, it is worth investing in a special oven thermometer to be sure the oven's temperature is accurate. Incorrect temperature settings will often lead to poor results. If your oven does not have a fan, you may need to increase cooking times slightly, but do not alter the temperatures given in the recipes.

TECHNIQUES & TROUBLESHOOTING

It is important that you follow the instructions correctly when baking. Understanding exactly what the following terms mean will help ensure you have the best results.

BEATING & WHISKING

Beat with a wooden spoon or electric beater when ingredients need to be combined briskly while still incorporating plenty of air. To whisk, use a large balloon whisk and beat the mixture quickly, lifting the whisk from the bowl and combining the ingredients in a fast, circular motion to incorporate a maximum amount of air. Plenty of electric beaters will do this for you.

FOLDING

You are told to fold when ingredients need to be combined gently, incorporating as much air into the mixture as possible. Use a large, metal spoon that will slice through the mixture easily. Touching the bottom of the bowl with the spoon, adopt a cutting motion through the center of the mixture, folding over when you reach the side of the bowl to unearth the pockets of flour and other dry ingredients.

MELTING CHOCOLATE

The best way of melting chocolate is probably in a double boiler, where one pan is designed to nestle into a slightly larger pan. If you don't have one, use a heatproof bowl placed over a smaller pan of barely boiling, water. Make sure the bowl does not touch the water. It is the gentle heat of the steam that will slowly melt the chocolate.

Dark chocolate should be stirred as little as possible, while milk and white chocolate melt better if stirred more frequently. Do not overheat and be careful not to let any of the hot water touch the melted chocolate, because this will cause the chocolate to seize up and turn grainy. If this happens, try beating in a dash of vegetable oil until the mixture is smooth. You can also melt chocolate slowly in a microwave on low power, stirring occasionally.

RUBBING IN

This is when a recipe requires you to rub ingredients together to a texture of, say, fine bread crumbs. Normally, it refers to rubbing butter into flour, and is easiest if the butter is cold and has been diced first. Just rub the pieces of butter into the flour in a large bowl using the fingertips and lifting the mixture at the same time, letting it fall back into the bowl as you rub. This stops it from clumping together and gives you the texture of fine bread crumbs.

IS IT DONE YET?

How you check that a baked item is "done" depends on the type of cake you are baking. For example, a brownie bake needs to have firmed up, but should not be risen and springy like many other cakes. This is to ensure that the typical fudgy texture so particular to brownies develops. With other cakes, signs to look for are shrinking back from the sides of the pan, firmness, and that the sponge springs back when touched lightly with the fingertips.

BROWNIES &
BLONDIES

PRALINE LEMON BLONDIES

These layered praline, cookie, and lemon blondies are chilled in the refrigerator and served cold with fresh raspberries. Try serving as a dessert for a summer lunch as a spin on the more traditional lemon cheesecake.

MAKES ABOUT 16 BLONDIES

BASE
10½ oz graham crackers
¼ lb (1 stick) butter, melted
Generous ⅓ cup finely ground praline

BLONDIES
11 tablespoons (1⅜ sticks) butter, plus extra for greasing
10½ oz white chocolate, broken into chunks
Scant ½ cup cream cheese
½ cup superfine sugar
3 eggs
3–4 drops of lemon extract
1 cup self-rising flour
Finely grated zest of 1 lemon
2 cups fresh raspberries, to serve

TO DECORATE
2–3 tablespoons roughly ground praline
Fresh mint sprigs

1. Preheat the oven to 350°F. Grease a deep 13 x 9-inch brownie pan and line the bottom with parchment paper.

2. For the base, place the graham crackers in the large bowl of a food processor and pulse until they turn to crumbs. Turn into a large bowl, pour in the melted butter, and stir until well coated. Stir in the ground praline, then turn into the prepared pan, pressing down well. Set aside in a cool place to set.

3. For the blondie, in a heavy saucepan over low heat, slowly melt the butter with the white chocolate, stir until smooth, then set aside to cool.

4. In a large bowl, beat the cream cheese with the sugar, then add the eggs one at a time, continuing to beat until smooth. Stir in the melted chocolate and lemon extract, followed by the flour and lemon zest.

5. Pour over the set cookie base and bake in the preheated oven for 35–40 minutes, until almost firm and golden. Let cool in the pan, then place in the refrigerator to chill.

6. Once cold, cut into squares, remove from the parchment paper, and lift out with a metal spatula. Serve with fresh raspberries, sprinkled with extra ground praline, and decorated with mint sprigs.

DOUBLE NUT BROWNIES

These classic chocolate brownies have both walnuts and pecans hidden beneath their crisp, sugary surface. Try replacing them with your favorite nuts to personalize your brownies.

MAKES 12–16 BROWNIES

½ lb (2 sticks) butter, plus extra for greasing

7 oz dark chocolate, broken into chunks

3 eggs

1 teaspoon vanilla extract

1 tablespoon strong espresso (or 1 tablespoon instant coffee dissolved in 1 tablespoon hot water)

Scant 1 cup superfine sugar

¾ cup all-purpose flour

½ teaspoon salt

⅔ cup roughly chopped walnuts

⅔ cup roughly chopped pecans

1. Preheat the oven to 350°F. Grease a 13 x 9-inch brownie pan and line the bottom with parchment paper.

2. In a small, heavy saucepan over low heat, slowly melt the butter with the chocolate, stir until smooth, then set aside to cool.

3. In a large bowl, beat the eggs with the vanilla extract, espresso, and sugar, followed by the melted chocolate. Add the flour and salt, and mix until well combined, then stir in both types of nuts.

4. Pour the brownie mixture into the prepared pan and bake in the preheated oven for 25–30 minutes. Be careful not to overcook—the sides should be firm but it should still be slightly soft in the center.

5. Let cool in the pan for 10 minutes, then cut into squares, remove from the parchment paper, and lift out carefully with a metal spatula. Serve slightly warm, or cool completely and store in an airtight container between layers of wax paper.

FROSTED COFFEE & MACADAMIA BROWNIES

MAKES 12–16 BROWNIES

BROWNIES

12 tablespoons (1½ sticks) butter,
   plus extra for greasing
6 oz dark chocolate, broken into
   chunks
1½ tablespoons very strong coffee
   (1½ tablespoons instant coffee
   dissolved in 1½ tablespoons
   boiling water)
2 large eggs
Generous ¾ cup superfine sugar
Generous ⅓ cup self-rising flour
Pinch of salt
⅔ cup roughly chopped
   macadamia nuts

FROSTING

5 tablespoons softened butter
1¾ cups confectioners' sugar, sifted
1 teaspoon ground cinnamon
1 tablespoon coffee extract
Generous ⅓ cup grated milk
   chocolate, to decorate

1. Preheat the oven to 400°F. Grease a 13 x 9-inch brownie pan and line the bottom with parchment paper.

2. In a small, heavy saucepan over low heat, slowly melt the butter and dark chocolate with the strong coffee, stir until smooth, then set aside to cool.

3. In a large bowl, beat the eggs with the sugar, followed by the melted chocolate and strong coffee. Add the flour and salt, and mix until well combined, then stir in the macadamia nuts.

4. Pour the brownie mixture into the prepared pan and bake in the preheated oven for about 20 minutes. The brownie should rise but still be soft in the center. Let cool completely in the pan.

5. To make the frosting, beat together the softened butter, confectioners' sugar, ground cinnamon, and coffee extract until smooth. Spread the frosting over the cooled brownie, then sprinkle with the grated chocolate. Cut into squares, remove from the parchment paper, and serve.

FESTIVE CRANBERRY BROWNIES

The vanilla, allspice, cranberries, and nuts in these chocolate brownies
will leave even the hardiest of humbugs in a festive mood!

MAKES 12–16 BROWNIES

14 tablespoons (1¾ sticks) butter,
    plus extra for greasing
5½ oz dark chocolate, broken into
    chunks
3 eggs
Scant 1 cup superfine sugar
Seeds scraped from 1 vanilla bean
1 teaspoon almond extract
1 cup all-purpose flour
Pinch of salt
1½ teaspoons ground allspice
¾ cup dried cranberries
⅓ cup crushed hazelnuts
3½ oz white chocolate, roughly
    chopped

1. Preheat the oven to 350°F. Grease a 13 x 9-inch brownie pan and line the bottom with parchment paper.

2. In a small, heavy saucepan over low heat, slowly melt the butter and chocolate, stir until smooth, then set aside to cool.

3. In a large bowl, beat the eggs with the sugar, vanilla seeds, and almond extract, followed by the melted chocolate. Add the flour, salt, and ground allspice, and mix until well combined, then stir in the cranberries, nuts, and white chocolate.

4. Pour the brownie mixture into the prepared pan and bake in the preheated oven for 25–30 minutes, until cooked but still slightly soft.

5. Let cool in the pan for at least 10 minutes, then cut into squares. Lift out carefully with a metal spatula. Serve slightly warm, or cool completely and store in an airtight container between layers of wax paper.

CHERRY CHEESECAKE BROWNIES

MAKES 12–16 BROWNIES

BROWNIE

7 tablespoon butter, plus extra
    for greasing
4 oz dark chocolate, broken into
    chunks
2 eggs
⅔ cup superfine sugar
Scant ½ cup all-purpose flour
¼ cup unsweetened cocoa
½ teaspoon salt
½ cup drained cherries canned in
    light syrup, roughly chopped, plus
    2 tablespoons of the syrup

CHEESECAKE

1 egg
⅔ cup cream cheese
Scant ⅔ cup mascarpone
⅓ cup superfine sugar
½ teaspoon vanilla extract
⅔ cup drained cherries canned in
    syrup, halved

1. Preheat the oven to 375°F. Grease a 9-inch square brownie pan and line the bottom with parchment paper.

2. First make the cherry brownie base. In a small, heavy saucepan over low heat, slowly melt the butter with the dark chocolate, stir until smooth, then set aside to cool.

3. In a large bowl, beat the eggs with the sugar, followed by the melted chocolate. Add the flour, unsweetened cocoa, and salt and mix until well combined. Stir in the roughly chopped cherries and the reserved syrup, and pour into the prepared brownie pan. Set aside.

4. Now make the cheesecake. In a separate bowl, beat together the egg, cream cheese, mascarpone, superfine sugar, and vanilla extract until smooth. Lightly spoon over the brownie mix, swirling the mixture with a spoon to produce a slight marbled effect. Now scatter over the halved cherries, swirling again to just combine.

5. Bake in the preheated oven for 20–25 minutes, until it has risen and is almost firm. Let cool in the pan, then cut into squares and remove from the parchment paper.

TIP
Make sure the cream cheese and mascarpone are at room temperature to produce a softer, smoother mixture.

ORANGE & ALMOND BLONDIES

Bring the tastes and aromas of the Mediterranean to your kitchen with these golden blondies, full of zesty orange and moist almonds. They make a wonderful, quick dessert served with a small glass of Amaretto liqueur.

MAKES 12–16 BLONDIES

11 tablespoons (1⅜ sticks) butter, plus extra for greasing
9 oz white chocolate, broken into chunks
3 eggs
½ cup packed light brown sugar
1 teaspoon orange extract
1 teaspoon almond extract
Grated zest of 1 orange
¾ cup self-rising flour
¾ cup ground almonds
½ cup slivered almonds, lightly toasted

1. Preheat the oven to 325°F. Grease a 9-inch square brownie pan and line the bottom with parchment paper.

2. In a small, heavy saucepan over low heat, slowly melt the butter with the white chocolate, stir it until smooth, then set aside to cool.

3. In a large bowl, beat the eggs with the sugar, orange extract, almond extract, and orange zest, followed by the melted chocolate. Add the flour and ground almonds, and mix until well combined.

4. Pour the mixture into the prepared pan, scatter over the slivered almonds, and bake in the preheated oven for 25–30 minutes, until almost firm and golden.

5. Let cool in the pan, then cut into squares, remove from the parchment paper, and lift out with a metal spatula. Serve slightly warm, or cool completely and store in an airtight container between layers of wax paper.

MIXED FRUIT & NUT FEAST BROWNIES

There are whole hazelnuts and plenty of raisins in these brownies, making the fruit and nut feast a real hit. Feel free to substitute for your favorite mix of nuts and dried fruit.

MAKES ABOUT 18 BROWNIES

½ lb (2 sticks) butter, plus extra for greasing

4 oz dark chocolate, broken into chunks

3½ oz milk chocolate, broken into chunks

3 eggs

⅔ cup superfine sugar

½ cup packed dark brown sugar

⅔ cup self-rising flour

Pinch of salt

⅔ cup raisins

14 candied cherries, chopped

⅔ cup whole blanched hazelnuts, lightly toasted

⅓ cup shredded coconut

1. Preheat the oven to 350°F. Grease a 13 x 9-inch brownie pan and line the bottom with parchment paper.

2. In a small, heavy saucepan over low heat, slowly melt the butter with the dark and milk chocolates, stir until smooth, then set aside to cool.

3. In a large bowl, beat the eggs with the sugars, followed by the melted chocolate. Add the flour and salt, and mix until well combined, then stir in the raisins, cherries, hazelnuts, and coconut.

4. Pour the brownie mixture into the prepared pan and bake in the preheated oven for about 25–30 minutes. The brownie should rise but still be slightly soft in the center.

5. Let cool in the pan for at least 10 minutes, then cut into squares, removed from the parchment, and lift out with a metal spatula. Serve slightly warm, or cool completely and store in an airtight container between layers of wax paper.

NOUGAT BLONDIES & BLUEBERRY COULIS

MAKES 12–16 BLONDIES

COULIS
⅔ cup fresh or frozen blueberries
2 tablespoons confectioners' sugar
½ teaspoon vanilla extract
3 tablespoons orange juice

BLONDIES
7 tablespoons butter, plus extra
   for greasing
8 oz white chocolate, broken into
   chunks
3 eggs
½ cup superfine sugar
½ teaspoon almond extract
¾ cup self-rising flour
3½ oz soft nougat, chopped

1. To make the coulis, place the blueberries in a small saucepan with the sugar, vanilla extract, and orange juice and heat gently until the sugar has dissolved and the fruit has collapsed. Set aside to cool, then store in the refrigerator.

2. Preheat the oven to 325°F. Grease a 9-inch square brownie pan and line the bottom with parchment paper.

3. In a small, heavy saucepan over low heat, slowly melt the butter with the white chocolate, stir until smooth, then set aside to cool.

4. In a large bowl, beat the eggs with the sugar and almond extract, followed by the melted chocolate. Add the flour and chopped nougat, and mix until well combined.

5. Pour into the prepared pan and bake in the preheated oven for 20–25 minutes, until almost firm and golden.

6. Let cool in the pan, then cut into squares, remove from the parchment paper, and lift out with a metal spatula. Serve with a spoonful of blueberry coulis.

BASIC BLONDIES

An adaptable basic white chocolate blondie recipe, it produces blondies
that are delicious as they are or with some added chopped nuts or
dried fruit. Why not try with chunks of dark chocolate for an impressive
black and white brownie?

MAKES ABOUT 16 BLONDIES

5 tablespoons butter, plus extra for
   greasing
10½ oz white chocolate, broken into
   chunks
3 eggs
½ cup superfine sugar
2 teaspoons vanilla extract
1¼ cup self-rising flour
Generous ½ cup white chocolate
   chips
Confectioners' sugar, to dust

1. Preheat the oven to 325°F. Grease a 9-inch square brownie pan and
line the bottom with parchment paper.

2. In a small, heavy saucepan over low heat, slowly melt the butter with
the white chocolate, stir until smooth, then set aside to cool.

3. In a large bowl, beat the eggs with the sugar and vanilla extract,
followed by the melted chocolate. Add the flour and chocolate chips,
and mix until well combined.

4. Pour into the prepared pan and bake in the preheated oven for about
20 minutes, until almost firm and golden.

5. Let cool in the pan, then cut into squares, remove from the parchment
paper, and lift out with a metal spatula. Dust with confectioners' sugar,
and store in an airtight container between layers of wax paper.

CHOC & ALMOND BROWNIES

Ground almonds replace the flour in these sophisticated, alternative-style brownies, making them gluten-free. They are perfect eaten warm or cold.

MAKES 12–16 BROWNIES

14 tablespoons (1¾ sticks) butter, plus extra for greasing
7 oz dark chocolate, broken into chunks
4 eggs
¾ cup superfine sugar
1 tablespoon Amaretto liqueur (optional)
2⅔ cups ground almonds
½ teaspoon salt

1. Preheat the oven to 350°F. Grease a 13 x 9-inch brownie pan and line the bottom with parchment paper.

2. In a small, heavy saucepan over low heat, slowly melt the butter with the chocolate, stir until smooth, then set aside to cool.

3. In a large bowl, beat the eggs with the sugar and Amaretto, if using, followed by the melted chocolate. Add the ground almonds and salt, and mix until well combined.

4. Pour into the prepared pan and bake in the preheated oven for 20–25 minutes, until it has risen and is firm.

5. Let cool in the pan, then cut into squares, remove from the parchment paper, and lift out with a metal spatula. Store in an airtight container between layers of wax paper.

AFTER-DINNER BROWNIES WITH GANACHE

GANACHE FROSTING

½ cup heavy cream

7 oz dark chocolate (minimum 80% cocoa), finely chopped

4 tablespoons butter, cubed

1 tablespoon cognac (optional)

BROWNIES

½ lb (2 sticks) butter, plus extra for greasing

3½ oz dark chocolate, broken into chunks

4 oz praline-flavored milk chocolate, broken into chunks

3 eggs

1 teaspoon coffee extract

1 cup packed dark brown sugar

⅔ cup self-rising flour

Pinch of salt

½ cup slivered almonds

1¼ cups lightly whipped cream, to serve (optional)

1. Preheat the oven to 375°F. Grease a shallow 13 x 9-inch brownie pan and line the bottom with parchment paper.

2. Make the ganache frosting. Pour the cream into a small saucepan and heat to boiling point. Place the chopped chocolate in a bowl and pour over the hot cream, beating with a balloon whisk, until the chocolate has melted. Stir in the pieces of butter until melted. Let cool and stir in the cognac, if using. Set aside.

3. To make the brownies, in a small, heavy saucepan over low heat, slowly melt the butter with the dark chocolate and praline chocolate, stir until smooth, then set aside to cool.

4. In a large bowl, beat the eggs and coffee extract with the sugar, followed by the melted chocolate. Add the flour and salt, and mix until well combined.

5. Pour the brownie mixture into the prepared pan, scatter over the slivered almonds, and bake in the preheated oven for about 35 minutes. The brownie should rise but still be slightly soft in the center.

6. Let cool completely in the pan, then cut into squares, remove from the parchment paper, and lift onto a cooling rack. Pour the ganache frosting over each brownie and allow to drizzle over the sides. Let set, then serve with a dollop of lightly whipped cream, if liked.

CHUNKY CHOC & BANANA BROWNIES

The combination of banana chips and chocolate in this wickedly delicious brownie is a marriage made in heaven!

MAKES 12–16 BROWNIES

½ lb (2 sticks) butter, plus extra for greasing
8 oz dark chocolate, broken into chunks
3 eggs
⅔ cup superfine sugar
½ cup packed dark brown sugar
⅔ cup self-rising flour
Pinch of salt
3½ oz milk chocolate, chopped
2¾ oz dried banana chips, roughly crushed
⅓ cup shredded coconut

1. Preheat the oven to 400°F. Grease a 13 x 9-inch brownie pan and line the bottom with parchment paper.

2. In a small, heavy saucepan over low heat, slowly melt the butter with the dark chocolate, stir until smooth, then set aside to cool.

3. In a large bowl, beat the eggs with the sugars, followed by the melted chocolate. Add the flour and salt, and mix until well combined, then stir in the chopped milk chocolate, banana chips, and coconut.

4. Pour the brownie mixture into the prepared pan and bake in the preheated oven for about 20 minutes. The brownie should rise but still be slightly soft in the center.

5. Let cool in the pan for at least 10 minutes, then cut into squares, remove from the parchment paper, and lift out with a metal spatula. Serve slightly warm, or cool completely and store in an airtight container between layers of wax paper.

CHOC CHESTNUT BROWNIES WITH CREAM

If you can find them, it's worth the extra expense of buying special French marrons glacés, or candied chestnuts. Combined with the unctuous cream topping, you are left with a really luxurious-tasting brownie.

MAKES 16–18 BROWNIES

BROWNIES
½ lb (2 sticks) butter, plus extra
   for greasing
8 oz dark chocolate, broken into
   chunks
3 eggs
⅔ cup superfine sugar
½ cup packed light brown sugar
⅔ cup self-rising flour
Pinch of salt
1⅓ cup sweetened chestnut puree
5½ oz cooked, peeled, and chopped
   chestnuts (8 oz fresh in their shell)

CHESTNUT CREAM
Generous 1 cup heavy cream
⅔ cup sweetened chestnut puree
4–5 marrons glacés, very thinly sliced
   (optional)

1. Preheat the oven to 400°F. Grease a 13 x 9-inch brownie pan and line the bottom with parchment paper.

2. In a small, heavy saucepan over low heat, slowly melt the butter with the dark chocolate, stir until smooth, then set aside to cool.

3. In a large bowl, beat the eggs with the sugars, followed by the melted chocolate. Add the flour and salt, and mix until well combined, then stir in the chestnut puree and chopped chestnuts.

4. Pour the brownie mixture into the prepared pan and bake in the preheated oven for about 25–30 minutes. The brownie should rise but still be slightly soft in the center.

5. Let cool in the pan for at least 10 minutes, then cut into squares, remove from the parchment paper, and lift out with a metal spatula.

6. Meanwhile, whip the cream in a large, clean bowl until it stands in soft peaks. Fold in the sweetened chestnut puree.

7. Serve the brownies slightly warm with a dollop of chestnut cream and scattered with the thinly sliced marrons glacés, if liked.

MARZIPAN & GOLDEN RAISIN BLONDIES

These golden blondies are studded with golden raisins and have a wonderfully moist and slightly chewy texture, thanks to the chopped marzipan scattered over the blondie mixture.

MAKES 16–18 BLONDIES

3 tablespoons brandy

⅔ cup golden raisins

1 tablespoon dark corn syrup

11 tablespoons (1⅜ sticks) butter, plus extra for greasing

9 oz white chocolate, broken into chunks

3 eggs

½ cup superfine sugar

1¼ cups all-purpose flour

5½ oz marzipan, chopped

2 tablespoons confectioners' sugar, to dust

1. Preheat the oven to 325°F. Grease a 13 x 9-inch brownie pan and line the bottom with parchment paper.

2. In a small, heavy pan over medium-low heat, warm the brandy with the raisins and syrup. Simmer gently for 2–3 minutes, then set aside for the raisins to plump and absorb the juices.

3. In a small, heavy pan over low heat, slowly melt the butter with the white chocolate, stir until smooth, then set aside to cool.

4. In a large bowl, beat the eggs with the sugar, followed by the melted chocolate. Add the flour and soaked raisins, and mix until well combined.

5. Pour the mixture into the prepared pan, scatter with the chopped marzipan, and bake in the preheated oven for about 20 minutes, until almost firm and golden.

6. Let cool in the pan, then cut into squares, remove from the parchment paper, and lift out with a metal spatula, Dust with sifted confectioners' sugar. Store in an airtight container between layers of wax paper.

MINT CHOCOLATE CHUNK BROWNIES

This grown-up brownie uses a green-colored mint syrup or liqueur. You can use a little water with a drop of green food coloring instead if you prefer.

MAKES 12–16 BROWNIES

BROWNIES
14 tablespoons (1¾ sticks) butter, plus extra for greasing

3½ oz dark chocolate, broken into chunks

7 oz dark mint-flavored chocolate, broken into chunks

3 eggs

½ cup superfine sugar

½ cup packed dark brown sugar

⅔ cup self-rising flour

½ teaspoon salt

TO DRIZZLE
1¼ cups confectioners' sugar

2 tablespoons green colored mint syrup or liqueur

1. Preheat the oven to 350°F. Grease a 13 x 9-inch brownie pan and line the bottom with parchment paper.

2. In a small, heavy saucepan over low heat, slowly melt the butter with the dark chocolate and half the mint-flavored chocolate, stir until smooth, then set aside to cool.

3. In a large bowl, beat the eggs with both the sugars, followed by the melted chocolate. Add the flour and salt, and mix until well combined, then stir in the remaining mint chocolate chunks.

4. Pour the brownie mixture into the prepared pan and bake in the preheated oven for about 25 minutes. The brownie should rise but still be slightly soft in the center. Let cool in the pan.

5. Stir the mint syrup or liqueur into the confectioners' sugar until completely smooth, then use a teaspoon to drizzle back and forth over the brownie. Let set, then cut into squares, remove from the parchment paper, and lift out with a metal spatula. Store in an airtight container between layers of wax paper.

BRUNCH BROWNIES

A great alternative to the typical chocolate variety, this brownie is full of goodness. Whether it's for breakfast on the run or a more leisurely brunch, this brownie will give you a satisfying kick-start that will leave you virtuous all day!

MAKES 12–16 BROWNIES

11 tablespoons (1⅜ sticks) butter, plus extra for greasing
2 tablespoons molasses
3 eggs
½ cup packed dark brown sugar
Generous 1 cup cream cheese
1 small apple, peeled and coarsely grated
Scant 1 cup coarsely grated pumpkin flesh
Scant 1 cup rolled oats
⅓ cup golden raisins
1 cup wholewheat flour
1 teaspoon baking soda
1 teaspoon baking powder
¼ cup bran
2 tablespoons sesame seeds

1. Preheat the oven to 350°F. Grease a 13 x 9-inch brownie pan and line the bottom with parchment paper.

2. In a small, heavy saucepan over low heat, slowly melt the butter, then stir in the molasses until smooth, then set aside to cool.

3. In a large bowl, beat the eggs with the sugar and cream cheese until smooth, then pour in the melted butter and molasses. Stir in the grated apple and pumpkin, followed by the oats and raisins. Add the flour, baking soda, baking powder, and bran, and mix until well combined.

4. Pour into the prepared pan, scatter with the sesame seeds, and bake in the preheated oven for about 30 minutes, until it has risen and is golden.

5. Let cool in the pan, then cut into squares, remove from the parchment paper, and lift out with a metal spatula. Serve slightly warm, or cool completely and store in an airtight container between layers of wax paper.

TIP
If you feel that it's not a brownie without chocolate, then stir ½ cup dark chocolate chips into the batter before baking.

SPONGE TOFFEE BROWNIES

The sponge toffee—which is sometimes called sponge candy, sea foam, fairy food candy, or honeycomb—melts into this chocolate creation during cooking, leaving you with a slightly chewy brownie that is difficult to resist.

MAKES 12–16 BROWNIES

½ lb (2 sticks) butter, plus extra for greasing
8 oz dark chocolate, broken into chunks
4 oz sponge toffee
3 eggs
Generous 1 cup superfine sugar
⅔ cup self-rising flour

1. Preheat the oven to 350°F. Grease a 13 x 9-inch brownie pan and line the bottom with parchment paper.

2. In a small, heavy saucepan over low heat, slowly melt the butter with the dark chocolate, stir until smooth, then set aside to cool.

3. Place two-thirds of the sponge toffee between 2 layers of wax paper and tap lightly with a rolling pin to break into small pieces. Break the remaining sponge toffee into shards and set aside for decoration.

4. In a large bowl, beat the eggs with the sugar, followed by the melted chocolate. Add the flour and mix until well combined.

5. Pour into the prepared pan and bake in the preheated oven for about 25 minutes. The brownie should rise but still be slightly soft in the center.

6. Let cool in the pan for at least 10 minutes, the cut into squares, remove from the parchment paper, and lift out with a metal spatula. Serve slightly warm with extra shards of sponge toffee, or cool completely and store in an airtight container between layers of wax paper.

PUMPKIN BLONDIES

These blondies are a delicious treat during fall, when pumpkins are readily available—and they are perfect for a Halloween party.

MAKES 16 BLONDIES

1 pumpkin, about 1 lb
½ lb (2 sticks) butter, plus extra
    for greasing
10 oz white chocolate, broken into
    pieces
1 cup cream cheese
⅔ cup superfine sugar
3 eggs
¾ cup all-purpose flour
1 teaspoon vanilla extract
3 tablespoons pumpkin seeds

1. Preheat the oven to 375°F. Grease a shallow 13 x 9-inch brownie pan and line it with parchment paper.

2. Cut off the top of the pumpkin, then scoop out the seeds and fibers from the pumpkin. Cut away the skin and cut the flesh into ½-inch dice.

3. In a small, heavy saucepan over low heat, slowly melt the butter with the chocolate, stir until smooth, then set aside to cool.

4. In a large bowl, beat the cream cheese with the cooled melted chocolate until softened. Gradually beat in the sugar, then the eggs. Add the flour and vanilla extract, and mix until well combined.

5. Pour half the mixture into the prepared pan and scatter with half the chopped pumpkin. Spoon over the remaining mixture, then scatter with the remaining pumpkin pieces and the pumpkin seeds.

6. Bake the blondies in the preheated oven for 25 minutes, until the surface feels almost firm and golden.

7. Let cool in the pan for at least 10 minutes, then cut into squares, remove from the parchment paper, and lift out with a metal spatula. Cool completely and store in an airtight container between layers of wax paper.

FROSTED BLACK FOREST BROWNIES

MAKES 12–16 BROWNIES

BROWNIES

14 tablespoons (1¾ sticks) butter, plus extra for greasing

8 oz dark chocolate, broken into chunks

3 eggs

½ cup superfine sugar

½ cup packed dark brown sugar

¾ cup self-rising flour

¼ cup unsweetened cocoa

Pinch of salt

1 cup drained Morello cherries canned in their juice or light syrup (reserve the liquid)

SYRUP

Scant ½ cup juice or light syrup reserved from the Morello cherries

2 tablespoons kirsch

¼ cup packed dark brown sugar

TO SERVE

1–1½ cup whipped cream

½–1 tablespoon confectioners' sugar

Seeds from ½ vanilla bean

24–32 fresh black cherries

1¾ oz dark chocolate, curled

1. Preheat the oven to 400°F. Grease a 13 x 9-inch brownie pan and line the bottom with parchment paper.

2. In a small, heavy saucepan over low heat, slowly melt the butter and dark chocolate, stir it until smooth, then set aside to cool.

3. In a large bowl, beat the eggs with the sugars, followed by the melted chocolate. Add the flour, unsweetened cocoa, and salt, and mix until well combined.

4. Pour the brownie mixture into the prepared pan, scatter over the Morello cherries, and bake in the preheated oven for 30–35 minutes, until almost firm. Let cool in the pan and then prick the surface all over with the tines of a fork.

5. Place the reserved juice from the cherries in a small pan with the kirsch and sugar. Heat gently to dissolve the sugar, then simmer for 2–3 minutes to create a thin syrup. Set aside to cool a little before pouring over the baked brownie. Let stand to soak in the syrup.

6. Pour the cream into a clean bowl with the confectioners' sugar and vanilla seeds. Using an electric beater, beat until the cream stands in soft peaks.

7. Cut the brownies into squares, remove from the parchment paper and lift onto a serving plate. Spoon over a generous dollop of cream and decorate attractively with the fresh cherries and chocolate curls.

GLUTEN-FREE CHOCOLATE BROWNIES

You don't have to be on a gluten-free diet to enjoy these chocolaty brownies—they are just as delicious as brownies made with regular flour.

MAKES ABOUT 18 BROWNIES

14 tablespoons (1¾ sticks) butter, plus extra for greasing

7 oz dark chocolate, broken into chunks

3 eggs

¾ cup packed light brown sugar

⅔ cup gluten-free flour

2 teaspoons gluten-free baking powder

7 oz milk chocolate, chopped

1⅔ cups walnut pieces

1. Preheat the oven to 375°F. Grease a 11 x 7-inch shallow baking pan and line the bottom with parchment paper.

2. In a small, heavy saucepan over low heat, slowly melt the butter with the dark chocolate, stir until smooth, then set aside to cool.

3. In a large bowl, beat together the eggs and sugar, then stir in the melted chocolate. Add the flour and baking powder, and mix until well combined. Add the chopped chocolate and walnut pieces, and fold the ingredients together gently.

4. Pour the mixture into the prepared pan and bake in the preheated oven for 30 minutes, until a sugary crust has formed on the surface but the mixture gives slightly underneath.

5. Let cool in the pan, then cut into squares and lift out with a metal spatula. Serve slightly warm, or let cool completely and store in an airtight container between layers of wax paper.

TIP
Chop the walnuts finely if you prefer, or substitute almonds or macadamia nuts for a milder flavor.

CHOC & PEANUT BUTTER BROWNIES

There's no need to choose between chocolate and peanut butter with these brownies—you've got both. A great choice for a birthday party, guaranteed to please young and old alike!

MAKES ABOUT 18 BROWNIES

14 tablespoons (1¾ sticks) butter, plus extra for greasing

4 oz dark chocolate, broken into chunks

Generous 1 cup chocolate and hazelnut spread

½ cup chunky peanut butter

3 eggs

Generous 1 cup superfine sugar

⅔ cup self-rising flour

1. Preheat the oven to 400°F. Grease a 13 x 9-inch brownie pan and line the bottom with parchment paper.

2. In a small, heavy saucepan over low heat, slowly melt the butter, dark chocolate, and chocolate spread, stir until smooth, then set aside to cool.

3. Warm the peanut butter in the microwave or a small pan. Melt slightly until soft enough to drizzle.

4. In a large bowl, beat the eggs with the sugar, followed by the melted chocolate. Add the flour and mix until well combined.

5. Pour the brownie mixture into the prepared pan and drizzle over the peanut butter haphazardly. Use the end of a teaspoon to swirl the mixtures together a little. Bake in the preheated oven for about 30 minutes. The brownie should rise but still be slightly soft in the center.

6. Let cool in the pan, then cut into squares, remove from the parchment paper, and lift out with a metal spatula. Serve slightly warm, or cool completely and store in an airtight container between layers of wax paper.

TRIPLE CHOC & ESPRESSO BROWNIES

Don't be fooled by the white chocolate layer and the milk chocolate chips; the rich chocolate and strong espresso flavors make this an extremely grown-up brownie!

MAKES ABOUT 16 BROWNIES

½ lb (2 sticks) butter, plus extra for greasing

8 oz dark chocolate, broken into chunks

3 eggs

2 tablespoons strong espresso-style coffee

⅔ cup superfine sugar

½ cup packed dark brown sugar

⅔ cup self-rising flour

Pinch of salt

Generous ½ cup milk chocolate chips

½ cup coarsely grated white chocolate

1. Preheat the oven to 400°F. Grease a 13 x 9-inch brownie pan and line the bottom with parchment paper.

2. In a small, heavy saucepan, slowly melt the butter with the dark chocolate, stir until smooth, then set aside to cool.

3. In a large bowl, beat the eggs with the espresso and sugars, followed by the melted chocolate. Add the flour and salt, and mix until well combined, then stir in the milk chocolate chips.

4. Pour half the brownie mixture into the prepared pan, then scatter over the grated white chocolate, pressing down gently with fingertips. Cover with the remaining brownie mixture and bake in the preheated oven for 20–25 minutes. The brownie should rise but still be slightly soft in the center. Let cool for at least 10 minutes before cutting into squares. Serve slightly warm, or cool completely and store in an airtight container between layers of wax paper.

TIP
Try this recipe with other flavored chocolates, such as dark mint or praline chocolate. You could also make a layer with chopped nuts or raisins.

MANGO & WHITE CHOCOLATE BLONDIES

A tropical-inspired recipe, these blondies include dried mango.
Serve with slices of fresh, ripe mango for maximum impact!

MAKES 12–16 BLONDIES

11 tablespoons (1⅜ sticks) butter,
   plus extra for greasing
9 oz white chocolate, broken into
   pieces
1 ripe mango, peeled and pitted
3 eggs
⅔ cup superfine sugar
Seeds scraped from 1 vanilla bean
1¼ cups self-rising flour
3 tablespoons chopped dried mango
   (optional)
Generous ½ cup white chocolate
   chips
Fresh mango, sliced, to serve
   (optional)

1. Preheat the oven to 325°F. Grease a 9-inch square brownie pan and line the bottom with parchment paper.

2. In a small, heavy saucepan over low heat, slowly melt the butter with the white chocolate, stir until smooth, then set aside to cool.

3. Place half of the mango in the small bowl of a food processor and pulse until pureed. Dice the remaining half.

4. In a large bowl, beat the eggs with the sugar, vanilla seeds, and pureed mango, followed by the melted chocolate. Add the flour, diced fresh mango, and the dried mango, if using, and mix until well combined.

5. Stir in the white chocolate chips, pour into the prepared pan, and bake in the preheated oven for about 30 minutes, until almost firm and golden.

6. Let cool in the pan, then cut into squares, remove from the parchment paper, and lift out with a metal spatula. Serve with the fresh mango slices, if liked. Store in an airtight container between layers of wax paper.

CRANBERRY BLONDIES

These moist white-chocolate blondies, packed with chunky pieces of white chocolate and ruby-red cranberries, are a terrific seasonal treat.

MAKES 20 BLONDIES

¼ lb (1 stick) butter, plus extra for greasing

7 oz white chocolate, broken into chunks

3 eggs

Scant 1 cup superfine sugar

1 teaspoon vanilla extract

1¼ cups all-purpose flour

1 teaspoon baking powder

⅔ cup dried cranberries

1. Preheat the oven to 350°F. Grease a 11 x 7-inch brownie pan and line with parchment paper, snipping diagonally into the corners so that the paper fits snugly over the bottom and up the sides of the pan.

2. In a small, heavy saucepan over low heat, melt the butter with half of the chocolate, stir until smooth, then set aside.

3. In a large bowl, beat the eggs, sugar, and vanilla followed by the melted chocolate. Add the flour and baking powder, and mix until well combined.

4. Chop the remaining chocolate and fold half of it into the chocolate mixture with half of the cranberries.

5. Pour the mixture into the prepared pan and sprinkle with the remaining chopped chocolate and cranberries. Bake in the preheated oven for 30–35 minutes, until the blondie has risen well. The top of the cake should be crusty and golden and the center still slightly soft.

6. Let cool in the pan, then lift the paper-lined cake out, peel away the paper, and cut into squares to serve. Store in an airtight container between layers of wax paper.

BARS, FINGERS & SQUARES

RASPBERRY JAM SANDWICH FINGERS

Bring the humble jam sandwich to a delicious new level with these delicious and slightly crumbly fingers.

MAKES 16 FINGERS

18 tablespoons (2¼ sticks) butter,
  plus extra for greasing
1⅔ cups self-rising flour
1 cup instant cornmeal
1⅔ cups ground hazelnuts
Finely grated zest of 1 orange
⅔ cup superfine sugar
2 large eggs, beaten
1 cup raspberry jam
3 tablespoons confectioners' sugar

1. Preheat the oven to 325°F. Grease an 11 x 7-inch baking pan and line it with parchment paper, snipping diagonally into the corners so that the paper fits snugly over the bottom and up the sides of the pan.

2. In a small saucepan over low heat, melt the butter. Set aside to cool.

3. In a large bowl, mix the flour with the cornmeal, hazelnuts, orange zest, and superfine sugar.

4. In a separate bowl, mix the eggs with the butter, then beat into the dry mix until smooth. Turn two-thirds of the mixture into the prepared pan and use a rubber spatula to level.

5. Spread with the jam and top with teaspoons of the remaining cake mixture, leveling slightly but leaving some gaps for the jam to bubble up through.

6. Sprinkle over the slightly lumpy confectioners' sugar, then bake in the preheated oven for 25–30 minutes, until golden.

7. Let cool in the pan for about 10 minutes, then lift out onto a cooling rack and peel away the parchment paper from underneath. Cut into fingers once cool and serve.

CHOCOLATE & APRICOT FINGERS

This is a sophisticated, bite-size finger with just the right amount of tangy apricot to cut through the richness of the chocolate. It would be perfect served with a strong Italian coffee as an after-dinner treat.

MAKES 16–20 FINGERS

7 tablespoons butter, plus extra for greasing

7 oz good-quality dark chocolate (minimum 70% cocoa)

½ cup slivered almonds

4 oz (about 32) amaretti cookies, chopped in half

Scant ½ cup thinly sliced, plumped dried apricots

1¾ oz orange-flavored dark chocolate, chopped

1. Grease an 11 x 7-inch baking pan.

2. In a small, heavy saucepan over low heat, slowly melt the butter and chocolate, stir until smooth, then set aside to cool.

3. In a small skillet over low heat, gently dry-fry the slivered almonds until lightly golden.

4. In a large bowl, stir together the amaretti, apricots, and orange-flavored chocolate, then pour over the melted chocolate. Mix gently but thoroughly enough for everything to be covered in melted chocolate.

5. Turn the mixture into the prepared pan and press down using a rubber spatula. Sprinkle over the slivered almonds, pressing down very lightly.

6. Place in the refrigerator for at least 45 minutes, until firm. Cut into small, thin fingers and serve with strong espresso-style coffee.

PEACH STRUDEL FINGERS

Phyllo pastry is perfect for making a simple, speedy, delicious strudel.
Just unfold and separate the sheets, then brush them with butter and
roll them around the lightly spiced peach and almond mixture.

MAKES 4 FINGERS

3 ripe peaches, pitted and thinly
    sliced
2 tablespoons superfine sugar, plus
    extra to decorate
2 tablespoons ground almonds
½ teaspoon ground cinnamon
2 tablespoons golden raisins
6 phyllo pastry sheets,
    12 x 7 inches each
3 tablespoons butter, melted
Sifted confectioners' sugar,
    to decorate
Whipped cream, crème fraîche,
    or ice cream, to serve

1. Preheat the oven to 350°F.

2. In a medium bowl, gently toss together the peaches with the sugar, ground almonds, cinnamon, and raisins.

3. Lay a sheet of pastry on a work surface, with the longest edge toward you, and brush it with a little of the melted butter. Following the longest edge, spoon a quarter of the peach mixture in a line down the center, stopping about 2 inches in from either end.

4. Fold the short sides of the pastry over the filling. Fold one long side over the filling, then roll up to enclose the filling completely. Repeat to make 3 more.

5. Cut the remaining pastry sheets in half. Brush the outside edges of the filled strudels with a little more butter, then roll them up in the remaining sheets of pastry. Brush each of the strudels with the remaining butter and place on a baking sheet.

6. Bake in the preheated oven for 10–13 minutes, until golden brown. Sprinkle with a little confectioners' sugar and serve warm with whipped cream, crème fraîche, or ice cream.

CHOCOLATE & DATE FINGERS

These simple, delicious chocolaty fingers will be a sure-fire success
at any cake sale, and they will be a hit at home, too.

MAKES 16 FINGERS

5 tablespoons butter, plus extra
    for greasing
1 cup chopped, pitted dates
3½ oz dark chocolate, broken
    into chunks
2 tablespoons dark corn syrup
1 teaspoon unsweetened cocoa
½ teaspoon vanilla extract
1½ cups crushed graham crackers
½ cup crushed shortbread
½ cup crushed pecans
5½ oz white chocolate, melted
    (optional)

1. Grease a 13 x 7-inch baking pan.

2. In a medium, heavy saucepan over low heat, melt the butter with the
dates, then add the chocolate, syrup, cocoa, and vanilla extract. Stir over
a gentle heat until the chocolate has melted.

3. In a large bowl, stir together the crushed cookies and pecans, then
pour over the melted chocolate mixture, mixing until well combined.

4. Pour the mixture into the prepared pan and use a rubber spatula to
press down and level. Let cool at room temperature before drizzling with
the melted white chocolate, if using. Set aside until the chocolate has set.

5. Cut into fingers to serve, or store in an airtight container.

CHOCOLATY PYRAMID SLICES

This no-bake cake is set in a tilted cake pan to create an interesting shape.

Best of all, the chopped fruit and milk chocolate are an irresistible combination.

MAKES 12 SLICES

Butter, for greasing
10½ oz milk chocolate, broken
   into chunks
Scant ½ cup evaporated milk
6 oz graham crackers (about
   25 crackers), broken into pieces
¾ cup roughly chopped, pitted dates,
   prunes, or dried apricots
1 tablespoon chopped mixed nuts
1¾ oz dark chocolate, broken
   into chunks (optional)

TIP
*If any pieces of cracker
come above the level of the
chocolate mixture, slice them
off once the cake has set,
so that it sits flat on
the plate.*

1. Grease a 7-inch square baking pan and line the bottom and three sides with plastic wrap.

2. In a small, heavy saucepan over low heat, melt the milk chocolate with the evaporated milk, stirring frequently, until the chocolate has melted. Transfer to a bowl and let cool, but do not let it set.

3. Stir in the pieces of crackers, dried fruit, and nuts. Prop up one side of the prepared pan on a box so that it sits at an angle of 45 degrees and the unlined side of the pan is uppermost. Spoon in the cake mixture and level the surface. Let stand until firm, then transfer to the refrigerator to set completely.

4. Remove the cake from the pan and peel away the plastic wrap. Melt the dark chocolate, and using a teaspoon, drizzle lines of melted chocolate over the pyramid, if liked. Let set again, then serve thinly sliced.

CRANBERRY & CORNFLAKE SQUARES

Here's a twist on a favorite breakfast cereal, with the cranberries and marshmallows making these rose-tinted squares a delicious afternoon treat.

MAKES ABOUT 12 SQUARES

7 tablespoons butter, plus extra
  for greasing
7 oz pink marshmallows
1 tablespoon cranberry jelly
5⅓ cups cornflakes
⅓ cup chopped dried cranberries

1. Grease an 11 x 7-inch baking pan and line the bottom with parchment paper. Cut out an extra sheet of parchment paper the same size as the pan.

2. In a large pan over low heat, slowly melt the butter, marshmallows, and cranberry jelly.

3. Remove the pan from the heat, pour in the cornflakes, and add the cranberries. Mix gently until thoroughly coated, then turn into the prepared baking pan.

4. Lay the sheet of parchment paper over the cornflake mix and press down firmly with the palm of the hand. Set aside in a cool place until completely cold.

5. Remove from the pan, peel away the parchment paper, and cut into squares to serve, or store in an airtight container.

PUFFED QUINOA & MUESLI BARS

In these bars, you will find quinoa, a cereal filled with essential amino acids, bran flakes, which is a great source of dietary fiber, and linseeds, which are high in omega-3 fatty acids. However, these bars are not only healthy—they are also delicious!

MAKES ABOUT 16 BARS

14 tablespoons (1¾ sticks) butter,
    plus extra for greasing
3 tablespoons honey
⅓ cup packed light brown sugar
⅓ cup brown rice flour
2 eggs, lightly beaten
1⅓ cups honey-coated puffed quinoa
2 cups unsweetened fruit and nut
    muesli
⅓ cup chopped dried apricots
1¼ cups unsweetened bran flakes
2 tablespoons brown linseeds

1. Preheat the oven to 350°F. Lightly grease a 9-inch square baking pan.

2. In a small heavy saucepan over low heat, melt the butter with the honey and brown sugar. Remove from the heat, pour into a large bowl, and beat in the flour and eggs.

3. Stir through the quinoa, muesli, apricots, bran flakes, and linseeds until well combined.

4. Turn the mixture into the prepared pan, pressing down evenly. Bake in the preheated oven for about 20 minutes, until firm and golden.

5. Let cool in the pan for 5–10 minutes, then cut into bars and lift onto a cooling rack to cool completely. Store in an airtight container.

TIP
You can substitute the honey-coated quinoa for the plain puffed kind, if liked. Add an extra tablespoon of sugar to keep the same level of sweetness.

COCONUT & CHERRY DREAM BARS

This is a cherry-topped variant on a favorite afternoon snack.
Its chewy texture is due to the mix of coconut and brown sugar
and will be difficult to resist!

MAKES ABOUT 16 BARS

7 tablespoons butter, plus extra for
   greasing
1¼ cups packed light brown sugar
¾ cup all-purpose flour, plus
   2 tablespoons
1⅓ cups shredded coconut
½ teaspoon baking powder
Pinch of salt
2 eggs, beaten
1 teaspoon vanilla extract
½ cup candied cherries, roughly
   chopped

1. Preheat the oven to 350°F. Grease a deep 11 x 7-inch baking pan.

2. In a medium saucepan over low heat, melt the butter. Add ⅓ cup of the brown sugar and ¾ cup all-purpose flour to the melted butter along with ⅓ cup of the coconut.

3. Turn the mixture into the prepared pan and press down evenly using your fingertips. Place in the preheated oven for 10 minutes. Remove and let cool for 5 minutes.

4. In a bowl, stir together the remaining sugar, flour, and coconut with the baking powder and salt, then combine with the eggs and vanilla extract. Pour onto the cooked layer and level with a rubber spatula.

5. Scatter the candied cherries over the top and return to the oven for 20 minutes more, until golden and it has slightly risen.

6. Let cool in the pan, then cut into bars.

CRANBERRY & APPLE BARS

You can make these fruity cereal bars with or without the lemony frosting drizzled over the top.

MAKES 12–16 BARS

CEREAL BAR

14 tablespoons (1¾ sticks) butter, plus extra for greasing

Scant ⅔ cup dark corn syrup

⅔ cup packed light brown sugar

⅔ cup applesauce

5 cups rolled oats

¾ cup dried cranberries, roughly chopped

Pinch of salt

1 teaspoon ground cinnamon (optional)

LEMON DRIZZLE

1–2 tablespoons lemon juice

1¼ cups confectioners' sugar

1. Preheat the oven to 350°F. Grease a 13 x 9-inch jelly roll pan.

2. In a large, heavy saucepan over a low heat, melt the butter with the syrup. Stir in the sugar, then remove from the heat and add the applesauce, oats, cranberries, salt, and cinnamon, if using. Stir until well combined.

3. Turn the mixture into the prepared pan, flatten with a rubber spatula, and bake in the preheated oven for about 35 minutes, until lightly golden. Cut into bars and let cool in the pan.

4. For the drizzle, mix together the lemon juice and confectioners' sugar until smooth.

5. Use a metal spatula to lift the bars onto a cooling rack before drizzling with the frosting. Let the frosting set before serving.

CHERRY & CHOCOLATE NUT SLICES

Although macadamia nuts taste wonderful alongside the cherries and chocolate, you can substitute them with hazelnuts, which will work equally well.

MAKES 9 SLICES

9 tablespoons (1⅛ sticks) butter, plus extra for greasing
7 oz dark chocolate, broken into chunks
½ cup dark corn syrup
12 oz gingersnaps
⅔ cup candied cherries, halved
⅔ cup roughly chopped, toasted macadamia nuts

1. Grease an 8-inch square, loose-bottom cake pan and line the bottom with parchment paper.

2. In a small, heavy saucepan over low heat, melt the butter with the chocolate and corn syrup, stir until smooth, then set aside.

3. Place half the gingersnaps in a food processor and process to fine crumbs. Roughly chop the remaining cookies, then add both to the melted chocolate mixture, along with the cherries and nuts. Mix until well combined.

4. Spoon the chocolate mixture into the prepared pan and let set in the refrigerator for 2 hours.

5. Remove the cake from the pan, peel off the parchment paper, and cut into slices.

SUGAR-FREE PEACHY BREAKFAST BARS

Have a delicious and nutritious start to the day with these no-added-sugar or fat, soft breakfast bars! The sweetness and moistness come from the dried fruit and peach puree.

MAKES 12–16 BARS

Butter for greasing
2 eggs
1 cup peach puree
Scant 1½ cups rolled oats
Scant ½ cup prunes
½ cup chopped dried apple
3 tablespoons chopped almonds
¼ cup chopped pecans
Scant ½ cup all-purpose flour
1 teaspoon ground cinnamon

1. Preheat the oven to 350°F. Grease a 13 x 9-inch nonstick baking pan.

2. In a large bowl, beat the eggs with the peach puree. Add the oats, prunes, apple, almonds, and pecans, and mix until well combined. Stir in the flour and ground cinnamon.

3. Turn the mixture into the prepared pan and bake in the preheated oven for about 20 minutes, until firm and lightly golden.

4. Let cool for about 5 minutes, then carefully turn out onto a cooling rack to cool completely. Cut into bars and store in an airtight container or wrapped in aluminum foil.

CRUMBLY RASPBERRY & OAT FINGERS

Just like a dessert crumble, these little cakes provide that delicious contrast between crispy chunks of crumble and bursts of tangy fruit.

MAKES 12–14 FINGERS

12 tablespoons (1½ sticks) butter, slightly softened and cut into small pieces, plus extra for greasing
¾ cup all-purpose flour
⅔ cup wholewheat all-purpose flour
2 cups rolled oats
¾ cup superfine sugar
Finely grated zest of 1 lemon
2 cups fresh or frozen raspberries
Confectioners' sugar, for dusting

1. Preheat the oven to 350°F. Grease a shallow 11 x 7-inch baking pan and line the bottom with parchment paper.

2. Put the butter, flours, and oats in a bowl and work with your fingers until the mixture makes a coarse crumble. Stir in the sugar and lemon zest.

3. Turn half the mixture into the pan and gently pat it down into an even layer. Scatter the raspberries on top and sprinkle with the remaining crumble mixture.

4. Bake in the preheated oven for about 1 hour, or until the topping is turning golden. Cut into fingers and let cool in the pan. Remove from the parchment paper, lift out with a metal spatula, and serve dusted with confectioners' sugar.

CHOCOLATE & PEANUT BUTTER BARS

These sweet chocolate-covered peanut treats will be a hit at any children's party. Use all dark or all milk chocolate if you prefer, or why not try it with a swirl of melted white chocolate?

MAKES 24 SMALL BARS

COOKIE BASE
¼ lb (1 stick) butter, plus extra for greasing
3½ oz milk chocolate, broken into chunks
½ cup smooth or chunky peanut butter
2⅓ cups crushed graham crackers
⅓ cup confectioners' sugar

TOPPING
2 tablespoons butter
3½ oz milk chocolate, broken into chunks
3½ oz dark chocolate, broken into chunks

1. Grease an 11 x 7-inch baking pan.

2. To make the cookie base, in a medium, heavy saucepan over low heat, melt the butter with the chocolate and peanut butter, then stir in the cookie crumbs and confectioners' sugar.

3. Pour the mixture into the prepared pan, level it with a rubber spatula, and place in the refrigerator for 15–20 minutes, or until firm.

4. For the topping, in a small, heavy saucepan over low heat, slowly melt the butter with the two chocolates, stirring until smooth. Once melted, pour over the cookie base and level using the back of a spoon.

5. Let set completely before cutting into bars. Lift out with a metal spatula and store in an airtight container.

WHITE CHOCOLATE & RAISIN BARS

Use your favorite unsweetened fruit and nut muesli for these white chocolate-coated bars. They are so delicious, it will be difficult to resist eating them all immediately.

MAKES 12–16 BARS

9 tablespoons (1⅛ sticks) butter, plus extra for greasing

2 tablespoons honey

⅓ cup superfine sugar

3½ cups unsweetened muesli

⅔ cup raisins

Pinch of ground allspice

9 oz white chocolate, broken into pieces

Seeds scraped from 1 vanilla bean

1. Preheat the oven to 325°F. Grease a 9½ x 7-inch baking sheet that is at least ¾ inch deep and line the bottom with parchment paper.

2. In a small, heavy saucepan over low heat, slowly melt the butter with the honey and sugar, stirring until the sugar has dissolved.

3. In a large bowl, mix the muesli with the raisins and allspice, then pour over the melted butter mixture. Mix until well combined and the muesli is thoroughly coated.

4. Turn the mixture into the prepared pan, pressing down with a rubber spatula, and bake in the oven for 25–30 minutes, until golden. Remove from the oven and let cool in the pan completely.

5. In a heatproof bowl set over a saucepan of barely simmering water, add the white chocolate and vanilla seeds and slowly melt.

6. Pour the melted chocolate over the cooked muesli bars in a thick layer and let cool completely before cutting into bars. Remove the parchment paper, lift out with a metal spatula, and serve or store in an airtight container between layers of wax paper.

JEWELED COOKIE BARS

Kids will love the garish colors of these jeweled bars, and they are guaranteed to brighten up any party! The topping ingredients can be used as a guideline—make yours as wild and wonderful as you like!

MAKES ABOUT 20 BARS

COOKIE BASE
18 tablespoons (2¼ sticks) butter, softened, plus extra for greasing
¾ cup confectioners' sugar
1 teaspoon salt
2¼ cups all-purpose flour
½ cup shredded, dried coconut
½ cup dried currants
Finely grated zest of ½ orange

TOPPING
7 oz white chocolate, melted
¼ cup chopped dried papaya
¼ cup chopped dried pineapple
¼ cup chopped dried apricots
¼ cup red and green candied cherries, quartered
¼ cup mixed candied peel, chopped
1 tablespoon silver balls (optional)

1. Preheat the oven to 350°F. Grease a 13 x 9-inch baking pan.

2. In a large bowl, beat together the butter, sugar, and salt until pale and creamy. Mix the flour, coconut, currants, and orange zest into the butter to form a soft dough.

3. Turn the mixture into the prepared pan and flatten with the fingertips. Bake in the preheated oven for 30–35 minutes, until lightly golden. Let cool in the pan.

4. Once cool, pour the melted white chocolate over the cookie base and use the back of a spoon to spread the chocolate so that the base is covered but the surface is uneven.

5. Mix the dried fruits in a small bowl and scatter over the white-chocolate covering, pushing down lightly. Sprinkle with silver balls, if using, making it as pretty as possible.

6. Let the chocolate set before cutting into small bars. Store in an airtight container between layers of wax paper.

PECAN SYRUP SQUARES

These syrupy squares are like a cookie-based version of pecan pie. They can also be made with a mixture of nuts, such as walnuts, almonds, and hazelnuts. Just roughly chop and substitute them for the traditional pecans.

MAKES 12–16 SQUARES

COOKIE BASE

7 tablespoons butter, softened, plus
   extra for greasing
1/3 cup superfine sugar
1 tablespoon vanilla sugar
1 large egg yolk
1 cup all-purpose flour
1/2 teaspoon baking powder
1/4 teaspoon ground cinnamon

TOPPING

2 eggs
1/4 cup packed light brown sugar
Scant 1/2 cup maple syrup
2 tablespoons heavy cream
1 1/4 cups roughly chopped pecans

1. Preheat the oven to 350°F. Grease a 13 x 9-inch baking pan and line the bottom with parchment paper.

2. In a large bowl, beat together the butter, superfine sugar, vanilla sugar, and the egg yolk, then mix in the flour, baking powder, and cinnamon.

3. Turn the mixture into the prepared pan and press down evenly to cover the bottom. Bake in the preheated oven for 12–15 minutes, until lightly golden. Remove from the oven and set aside, then lower the temperature to 325°F.

4. For the topping, beat the eggs with the brown sugar, then stir in the maple syrup, heavy cream, and pecans. Pour the mixture over the cookie base and return to the oven for 20–25 minutes, until golden and bubbling.

5. Let cool in the pan, then cut into squares, remove from the parchment paper, and lift out with a metal spatula. Store in an airtight container between layers of wax paper.

SUNFLOWER & PUMPKIN POWER BARS

The aromas alone of these bars baking should be enough to give you a boost! They are dairy-free and power packed with enough fruit and seeds to leave you full of energy.

MAKES ABOUT 18 BROWNIES

Butter for greasing
2 tablespoons dark corn syrup
¼ cup maple syrup
2 tablespoons pumpkin oil
¼ cup vegetable oil
⅓ cup pumpkin seeds
⅓ cup sunflower seeds
1⅔ cups rolled oats
⅓ cup dried currants
¼ cup dried apple, finely chopped
2 tablespoons packed light brown sugar
Pinch of salt
2 tablespoons chopped unsalted peanuts
¼ cup dark chocolate chips

1. Preheat the oven to 350°F. Grease an 11 x 7-inch baking pan and line the bottom with parchment paper.

2. In a small, heavy saucepan over low heat, heat the corn syrup, maple syrup, pumpkin oil, and vegetable oil until runny.

3. In a large bowl, mix the pumpkin seeds and sunflower seeds with the oats, currants, apple, sugar, salt, and peanuts. Pour over the warmed honey mixture and mix until well combined.

4. Turn into the prepared pan, pushing down to fill the pan evenly. Scatter over the chocolate chips, pressing down lightly, and bake in the preheated oven for 20–25 minutes, until golden brown.

5. Let cool for 10 minutes before marking into bars with a sharp knife. Carefully lift onto a cooling rack with a metal spatula and let cool completely.

TIP
The pumpkin oil gives these bars an extra nutty taste. If you cannot find it, then replace it with 2 extra tablespoons of vegetable oil.

CRUNCHY FIG & APPLE SQUARES

These layered squares have a crisp pastry base that is topped with a fruity fig and apple mixture. Sandwich it all in with a crunchy nut crumble topping, bake until golden, and just try to stop them being devoured in moments!

MAKES ABOUT 24 SQUARES

PASTRY DOUGH
¼ lb (1 stick) butter, plus extra for greasing
2 tablespoons superfine sugar
2 tablespoons beaten egg
1½ cups all-purpose flour, plus extra for dusting

FRUIT LAYER
1–2 apples, peeled, cored and diced
1 cup dried figs
2 tablespoons apple juice
¼ cup packed dark brown sugar

CRUNCHY TOPPING
1 cup all-purpose flour
½ cup granulated sugar
⅔ cup mixed chopped nuts
7 tablespoons butter, melted

1. Preheat the oven to 400°F. Grease a 13 x 9-inch jelly roll pan and line the bottom with parchment paper.

2. For the dough, in a large bowl, beat the butter, sugar, and egg together until pale and creamy. Mix in the flour to form a soft, but rollable dough, adding an extra tablespoon of flour if necessary.

3. Roll out the dough on a lightly floured surface and lay over the bottom of the pan. Set aside to rest in the refrigerator.

4. For the fruit layer, in a small saucepan over low heat, place the diced apple with the figs, apple juice, and brown sugar, and cook gently for about 5 minutes, until the apple softens but holds its shape.

5. To make the topping, in a bowl combine the flour, sugar, and nuts with the melted butter and mix to form a coarse bread-crumb consistency.

6. Take the jelly roll pan from the refrigerator and spread the fruit mixture over the pastry.

7. Sprinkle over the crunchy nut topping and bake in the preheated oven for 20–25 minutes, until crisp and golden. Let cool in the pan, then cut into squares, lift out with a metal spatula, and serve.

PRUNE & ORANGE SLICES

Wrap up these rich, dark chocolate slices to make a delightful gift, or serve with strong coffee as an after-dinner treat, or when cravings demand!

MAKES ABOUT 24 SLICES

14 tablespoons (1¾ sticks) butter

7 oz orange-flavored dark chocolate, broken into chunks

5½ oz milk chocolate, broken into chunks

7 oz shortbread

Finely grated zest of 1 orange

1 cup chopped prunes

2 tablespoons chopped candied orange peel

½ cup white chocolate chips

1. Line a 13 x 9-inch baking pan with a large sheet of plastic wrap, with enough extra to fold over the top.

2. In a medium, heavy saucepan over low heat, slowly melt the butter with the dark chocolate and milk chocolate, stir until smooth, then set aside to cool.

3. Place the shortbread in a plastic bag and tap with a rolling pin to break up into pieces.

4. Stir the orange zest, prunes, candied peel, and cookie pieces into the melted chocolate and stir well until thoroughly coated. Stir in the white chocolate chips.

5. Turn the mixture into the prepared pan and press down gently into the pan to cover the bottom but not so much that it is completely smooth. Cover the surface with the plastic wrap and place in the refrigerator for at least an hour, or until cold and hardened.

6. Turn out onto a cutting board and cut into slices. Store in an airtight container between layers of wax paper.

TOFFEE APPLE BARS

MAKES 12–16 BARS

APPLE TOPPING

7 tablespoons butter, plus extra
   for greasing

6–8 apples, peeled, cored, and sliced

1 cup packed dark brown sugar

¼ cup lemon juice

PASTRY DOUGH

2½ cups all-purpose flour, plus extra
   for dusting

12 tablespoons (1½ sticks) butter,
   diced

¼ cup superfine sugar

Pinch of salt

3 large egg yolks

2 tablespoons crème fraîche, or
   1 tablespoon sour cream mixed
   with 1 tablespoon whipping cream

1. Preheat the oven to 375°F. Grease a 13 x 9-inch jelly roll pan.

2. In a large skillet over low heat, melt the butter, then add the apple slices. Sprinkle over the sugar and lemon juice and cook for about 45 minutes, carefully turning the apples in the hot syrup from time to time. Set aside to cool.

3. Meanwhile, prepare the pastry dough. Place the flour in a large bowl and use your fingertips to rub in the butter until the mixture resembles fine bread crumbs. Stir in the sugar and salt.

4. Add the egg yolks and crème fraîche to the bread-crumb mixture and use the blunt side of a knife to mix the pastry in a cutting motion. Bring together into a ball, wrap in plastic wrap, and place in the refrigerator for 30 minutes.

5. Once cool enough to handle, arrange the apple pieces in lines over the bottom of the prepared pan. Drizzle over 1–2 tablespoons of the syrup and reserve the rest.

6. Roll out the pastry dough on a lightly floured surface to the same measurements as the prepared pan and lift carefully into the pan, tucking in the sides to seal in the caramelized apple. Bake in the preheated oven for 25–30 minutes, until the pastry is crisp and golden.

7. Let cool in the pan for 10–15 minutes before turning upside down onto a cooling rack to cool completely. Once cold, transfer to a cutting board and cut into bars. Serve hot or cold with the remaining syrup.

COCONUT & HAZELNUT BARS

Coconut and hazelnut are combined to make a delicious base, which is then topped with a strawberry jelly mixture to make a truly tempting afternoon treat.

MAKES 18 BARS

6 tablespoons butter or sunflower margarine, chilled and diced, plus extra for greasing
½ cup shredded, dried coconut
Scant 1½ cups all-purpose flour
3 tablespoons packed light brown sugar
⅔ cup ground hazelnut
1 egg yolk mixed with 2 tablespoons water
1 cup reduced-sugar strawberry jelly
2 eggs
¼ cup superfine sugar

ICING

14 tablespoons (1¾ sticks) butter
2 cups sifted confectioners' sugar
7 oz dark chocolate, melted
½ cup roughly chopped hazelnuts, to decorate

1. Preheat the oven to 350°F. Grease a 9½ x 7-inch baking pan and line the bottom with parchment paper.

2. Pour boiling water over the dried coconut and let soak for 10 minutes.

3. In a large bowl, rub together the flour and butter or margarine until it forms bread crumbs, then stir in the brown sugar. Add the ground hazelnuts and the egg yolk mixture and stir in to form a dough. Press the dough into the bottom of the prepared pan.

4. In a bowl, mix together the jelly, eggs, and superfine sugar. Drain the coconut, if using, and add to the jelly mixture. Spoon or pour onto the cookie base.

5. Bake in the preheated oven for 30 minutes, until the base is cooked. Remove and set aside to cool in the pan.

6. To make the icing, in a large bowl beat the butter and confectioners' sugar until creamy. Gradually add the melted chocolate, beating continuously. When well combined, remove the base from the parchment paper and lift out with a metal spatula. Spoon the frosting over the base and spread evenly using a metal spatula. Sprinkle with the chopped hazelnuts, then cut into bars. Store in an airtight container.

"COOKIES & CREAM" FINGERS

These fingers are for only the sweet-toothed! Put a few of these pretty, layered fingers into an attractive box and decorate with a ribbon for a novel gift.

MAKES ABOUT 20 FINGERS

14 tablespoons (1¾ sticks) butter, plus extra for greasing

14 oz cream-filled chocolate sandwich cookies

6 oz white chocolate, broken into chunks

1¾ cups (14-oz can) sweet condensed milk

½ cup golden raisins

1. Preheat the oven to 350°F. Grease an 11 x 7-inch baking pan and line the bottom with parchment paper

2. In a small saucepan over low heat, melt half of the butter. Put half of the chocolate sandwich cookies into a food processor and process until they resemble fine bread crumbs.

3. Put the cookie crumbs into a bowl and pour over the melted butter, stirring until the crumbs are well coated. Turn the mixture into the prepared pan, cover with a sheet of wax paper, and push flat with the palms of the hands.

4. Remove the wax paper. Bake in the preheated oven for about 12 minutes, then set aside to cool.

5. In a small, heavy saucepan over low heat, slowly melt the white chocolate with the condensed milk and remaining butter. Simmer for a minute or two, then remove from the heat and set aside to cool.

6. Break up the remaining cookies into large chunks with your hands and stir into the white chocolate mixture along with the raisins. Pour over the cookie base, level, and place in the refrigerator for several hours, but preferably overnight, to set properly. Serve chilled, cut into fingers.

MAPLE & MACADAMIA BARS

This sticky tart is a macadamia take on the traditional pecan pie. It is delicious served warm with vanilla ice cream, or cold as an afternoon snack.

MAKES 12–16 BARS

PASTRY DOUGH

7 tablespoons butter, plus extra
   for greasing
1⅔ cups all-purpose flour, plus extra
   for dusting
¼ cup superfine sugar
1 tablespoon maple syrup
3–4 tablespoons cold water

TOPPING

1 generous cup macadamia nuts
3 eggs
¼ cup superfine sugar
3½ tablespoons butter, melted
2 tablespoons dark corn syrup
¾ cup maple syrup
1 teaspoon vanilla extract
Pinch of salt

1. Preheat the oven to 350°F. Grease a 13 x 9-inch baking pan and line the bottom with parchment paper.

2. To make the pastry dough, put the flour into a bowl and rub in the butter with your fingertips until the mixture resembles fine bread crumbs. Stir in the sugar and pour in the maple syrup and just enough cold water to bind the mixture to a soft, smooth dough. Roll into a ball, wrap in plastic wrap, and refrigerate for 20 minutes.

3. Meanwhile, put the macadamia nuts into a food processor and process until roughly chopped.

4. Roll out the pastry on a lightly floured surface and line the bottom and sides of the prepared pan, trimming the edges neatly.

5. To make the topping, in a large bowl, beat the eggs with the superfine sugar and butter. Beat in the corn syrup, maple syrup, vanilla extract, and salt. Stir in the macadamia nuts and pour the mixture over the pastry dough.

6. Bake in the preheated oven for 25–30 minutes, until crisp and golden. Let cool in the pan, then cut into bars, remove from the parchment paper, and lift out with a metal spatula. Serve warm or cold.

WHITE CHOCOLATE CRACKLES

A great standby recipe, these squares can be rustled up in a matter of minutes.
If you are making these for children, you might want to leave out the pine nuts.

MAKES 8–10 SQUARES

4 tablespoons butter
8 oz white chocolate, broken into
  chunks
Scant 1½ cups sweet condensed milk
4 cups crispy rice cereal
⅓ cup pine nuts

1. Line the bottom of a 9½ x 7-inch baking pan with parchment paper.

2. In a small, heavy saucepan, slowly melt the butter with the chocolate, stir until smooth, then set aside to cool for 10 minutes.

3. In a large bowl, stir together the melted chocolate with the condensed milk, then fold in the rice cereal and pine nuts. Spoon into the prepared pan, level the surface, and let stand until hard—don't put the pan in the refrigerator or the cereal will become soggy.

4. Remove from the pan, peel away the parchment paper, and cut into squares to serve.

MOSAIC BARS

A scattering of broken creamy white and milk chocolate candy bars make these simple bars attractive and fun. You can use cinnamon or allspice instead of ginger, or leave the spice out altogether if you like.

MAKES 36 BARS

4 tablespoons butter, cut into pieces, plus extra for greasing

1½ cups all-purpose flour, plus extra for dusting

1 teaspoon ground ginger

⅓ cup packed dark brown sugar

3 tablespoons dark corn syrup

1 egg yolk

5 oz thin milk chocolate bar, broken into pieces

5 oz thin white chocolate bar, broken into pieces

1. Preheat the oven to 350°F and grease a baking sheet.

2. Put the flour and ginger in a food processor. Add the butter and process until the mixture resembles bread crumbs. Add the sugar, corn syrup, and egg yolk, and process until the mixture starts to bind together.

3. Turn the dough out onto a lightly floured surface and roll out to a 9½-inch square. Place on the prepared baking sheet and chill for at least 30 minutes.

4. Scatter the chocolate pieces over the cookie dough. Push a rolling pin firmly over the broken chocolate to press it into the dough a little.

5. Bake in the preheated oven for 8–10 minutes, then let stand on the baking sheet until almost cool. Cut the square in half, then cut each half into 18 bars. Lift onto a cooling rack to cook completely. Store in an airtight container.

TIP

If you like, experiment with the decoration, using nonpareils or sugar-coated chocolate candies in place of the broken chocolate pieces.

BREAKFAST CEREAL BARS

These are the perfect store-cupboard treat to have to hand for those
busy days when you just don't have enough time for a proper breakfast.
Yummy and healthy, these are the perfect breakfast standby.

MAKES 16 BARS

7 tablespoons butter, softened, plus
  extra for greasing
2 tablespoons packed light brown
  sugar
2 tablespoons dark corn syrup
⅔ cup millet flakes
⅓ cup quinoa
½ cup dried cherries or cranberries
½ cup golden raisins
3 tablespoons sunflower seeds
2 tablespoons sesame seeds
2 tablespoons linseeds
½ cup shredded coconut
2 eggs, lightly beaten

1. Preheat the oven to 350°F. Grease an 11 x 7-inch shallow baking pan
and line the bottom with parchment paper.

2. In a large bowl, beat together the butter, sugar, and syrup until creamy.
Add all the remaining ingredients and beat well until combined.

3. Turn into the prepared pan and level the surface with the back of a
spoon. Bake in the preheated oven for 35 minutes, until deep golden.
Let cool in the pan.

4. Turn out onto a cutting board, peel away the parchment paper, and
carefully cut into 16 bars. Store in an airtight container.

TIP
*These crumbly breakfast
bars are a much healthier
alternative to store-bought
cereal bars. Not only are they
ideal for quick breakfasts,
they make great snacks or
lunch box fillers, too.*

CHOCOLATE-DIPPED APRICOT BARS

MAKES 12–16 BARS

14 tablespoons (1¾ sticks) butter,
 plus extra for greasing
3 tablespoons apricot jelly
1 cup chopped dried apricots
2 tablespoons water
3 cups rolled jumbo oats
½ cup packed light brown sugar
1⅓ cups wholewheat or white
 all-purpose flour
2 teaspoons baking powder
3 tablespoons honey
10½ oz milk or dark chocolate,
 broken into chunks

1. Preheat the oven to 350°F. Grease a 13 x 9-inch baking pan and line the bottom with parchment paper.

2. In a small saucepan over low heat, heat the apricot jelly with the apricots and 2 tablespoons of water until the jelly melts. Simmer gently for 3–4 minutes, then set aside to cool.

3. In a large bowl, mix the rolled jumbo oats with the sugar, flour, and baking powder.

4. In a large, heavy saucepan over low heat, melt the butter with the honey, then stir in the oat mixture. Turn half of the mixture into the prepared pan and press down with the palm of the hand.

5. Spoon over the sticky apricots, then cover evenly with the remaining oat mixture. Press down firmly and bake in the oven for 25–30 minutes, until golden and firm.

6. Let cool in the pan for about 10 minutes, then cut into bars, remove from the parchment paper, and lift onto a cooling rack with a metal spatula. Let cool completely.

7. In a heatproof glass bowl set over a saucepan of barely simmering water, slowly melt the chocolate. Dip both ends of each bar into the melted chocolate and return to the cooling rack for the chocolate to set. Store in an airtight container.

SHORTBREAD & PEANUT CARAMELS

MAKES 16–20 BARS

SHORTBREAD BASE

18 tablespoons (2¼ sticks) butter, softened, plus extra for greasing
2 tablespoons chunky peanut butter
¾ cup confectioners' sugar
½ teaspoon salt
2½ cups all-purpose flour
Finely grated zest of ½ lemon

TOPPING

12-oz jar dolce de leche, or good-quality caramel sauce
⅔ cup roughly chopped unsalted peanuts
5½ oz milk chocolate
5½ oz white chocolate

TIP

Try substituting the peanuts for any of your favorite nuts— Brazil nuts or hazelnuts will be equally delicious. The chocolates used for the topping can also be changed—how about orange- or praline-flavored chocolate?

1. Preheat the oven to 350°F. Grease a 9-inch square baking pan, at least ¾ inch deep, and line the bottom with parchment paper.

2. In a large bowl, beat together the butter, peanut butter, sugar, and salt until pale and creamy. Mix the flour and lemon zest into this mixture to form a soft dough.

3. Turn the mixture into the prepared pan and flatten with your fingertips. Prick the surface all over with the tines of a fork. Bake in the preheated oven for 30–35 minutes, until light golden. Let cool.

4. Once the shortbread base has cooled, spoon over the dolce de leche or caramel sauce, spreading it evenly with the back of the spoon. Scatter over the chopped peanuts and set aside.

5. In a heatproof glass bowl set over a saucepan of barely simmering water, heat the milk chocolate until just melted, stirring occasionally. Melt the white chocolate in the same way in a separate bowl.

6. Pour the milk chocolate in a thin layer over the peanuts to completely cover. Drizzle the white chocolate over the top, pouring thinly from side to side. Use a toothpick to swirl the two chocolates together attractively. Set aside in a cool place for the chocolate to set completely, then cut into bars and remove from the parchment paper.

FRESH LEMON SQUARES

TIP
You can replace the lemon zest and juice in this recipe with the zest of 2 limes and 6 tablespoons of lime juice.

Sugary sweet with the zesty taste from the lemon, these shortbread-style slices are sure to become a family favorite.

MAKES 36 SQUARES

18 tablespoons (2¼ sticks) butter, softened, plus extra for greasing
⅔ cup confectioners' sugar
1 teaspoon vanilla extract
2 cups all-purpose flour
4 eggs
Scant 1 cup granulated sugar
Grated zest of 1 lemon
Generous ⅓ cup lemon juice

1. Preheat the oven to 375°F. Grease a 13 x 9-inch shallow baking pan and line the bottom with parchment paper.

2. In a large bowl, beat the butter, ⅓ cup of the confectioners' sugar, and the vanilla extract until light and creamy. Sift in the flour and fold, a little at a time, into the creamed mixture until completely incorporated.

3. Turn the mixture into the prepared pan and spread it to make the surface even. Bake in the preheated oven for 20 minutes.

4. Meanwhile, put the eggs, granulated sugar, lemon zest, and lemon juice into a separate bowl. Stir to blend the ingredients but do not beat. Pour the mixture over the baked pastry layer. Return the pan to the oven and bake for 18–22 minutes more, until the topping is set and lightly brown.

5. Sift the remaining confectioners' sugar over the warm cake to cover it generously. Cut the cake into squares. Remove from the parchment paper and pan when cool.

MAPLE SYRUP OAT BARS

Not only is maple syrup the most natural form of sweetener there is, it also avoids the sugar highs and lows of other sweeteners. These bars make a perfect mid-morning snack.

MAKES 12 BARS

¾ cup sunflower margarine, plus 2 tablespoons, plus extra for greasing
Scant ½ cup maple syrup
⅔ cup packed light brown sugar
3⅔ cups rolled oats

1. Preheat the oven to 350°F. Grease a 6½ x 10 x 1½-inch baking pan and line it with parchment paper, snipping it diagonally in the corners so it fits snugly over the bottom and up the sides.

2. In a medium saucepan over medium heat, melt the margarine. Stir in the maple syrup and sugar, and simmer until the sugar is mostly dissolved. Remove from the heat and stir in the oats.

3. Spoon the mixture into the prepared pan and bake in the preheated oven for 25 minutes.

4. Let cool in the pan for a few minutes, then cut into bars while the mixture is still warm. Remove from the parchment paper and lift out with a metal spatula when cold. Store in an airtight container.

CARAMEL PINE NUT SLICES

MAKES 12 SLICES

9 tablespoons (1⅛ sticks) unsalted
   butter, softened, plus extra
   for greasing
⅓ cup superfine sugar, plus extra
   for dusting
1 cup all-purpose flour
Generous ⅓ cup rice flour
Pinch of salt
7 oz dark chocolate, broken into
   chunks

CARAMEL

3½ tablespoons butter
¼ cup packed light brown sugar
1¼ cups (14-oz can) sweetened
   condensed milk
½ cup pine nuts

1. In a large bowl, beat together the butter and sugar until pale and creamy. Sift in the flour, rice flour, and salt, and mix together to form a soft dough. Shape the dough into a flat round, wrap in plastic wrap, and chill for 30 minutes.

2. Preheat the oven to 375°F. Grease an 8-inch square baking pan and line with parchment paper, snipping diagonally into the corners to fit snugly and allowing the paper to overhang the sides of the pan.

3. Roll out the dough on a lightly floured surface and press into the prepared pan, smoothing it as flat as possible. Bake in the preheated oven for 20–25 minutes, until golden. Let cool.

4. Make the pine nut caramel. In a heavy saucepan over low heat, add the butter, sugar, and condensed milk, and heat gently, stirring constantly, until the butter has melted and the sugar has completely dissolved. Increase the heat and bring to a boil, beating constantly for up to 5 minutes, until the mixture thickens.

5. Remove the saucepan from the heat, stir in the pine nuts, and pour the mixture over the shortbread layer. Let stand until set. Chill for 2 hours until really firm.

6. In a heatproof bowl set over a saucepan of barely simmering water, add the chocolate and stir until melted. Pour over the caramel layer and spread flat with a metal spatula. Once set, remove the cake from the pan, peel away the parchment paper, and cut into slices.

SHEET CAKES

BANANA TOFFEE SHEET CAKE

This sheet cake has a moist, banana sponge base, topped with layers of toffee sauce, fresh bananas, and softly whipped cream—and what better way to finish it all off than with a dusting of grated chocolate?

MAKES 12–16 PORTIONS

SPONGE

12 tablespoons (1½ sticks) butter, softened, plus extra for greasing
¾ cup packed light brown sugar
3 eggs, beaten
1½ cups self-rising flour
¼ teaspoon ground cinnamon
1 teaspoon baking powder
2 ripe bananas, mashed
1–2 tablespoons milk

TOFFEE SAUCE

1⅓ cups sweet condensed milk
5 tablespoons butter
⅓ cup superfine sugar
3 medium bananas, sliced
1 cup heavy cream
⅓ cup coarsely grated milk chocolate (optional)

1. Preheat the oven to 350°F. Grease a deep 13 x 9-inch baking pan and line the bottom with parchment paper.

2. In a large bowl, beat together the butter and sugar, then add the eggs, flour, ground cinnamon, and baking powder, and beat until well combined. Fold through the mashed banana and milk.

3. Turn into the prepared pan, using a rubber spatula to level the surface. Bake in the preheated oven for about 30 minutes, until it has risen and is springy. Cool in the pan for 5–10 minutes, then turn onto a cooling rack. Peel away the parchment paper and cool completely.

4. To make the toffee sauce, pour the condensed milk into a saucepan with the butter and sugar and heat gently, stirring frequently until the sugar has dissolved. Simmer gently until thick and golden. Set aside to cool a little—it needs to be warm enough to spread, but not too hot.

5. Spread the toffee sauce over the sponge base, let cool, and then top with the sliced bananas.

6. Whip the cream until it forms soft peaks and cover the banana-toffee layer. Sprinkle with the grated chocolate, if using, and serve in thick slabs.

FROSTED SPICED GINGERBREAD

MAKES ABOUT 16 SQUARES

SPONGE

14 tablespoons (1¾ sticks) butter, plus extra for greasing

1¼ cups milk

⅓ cup dark corn syrup

1 scant ½ cup molasses

¾ cup packed dark brown sugar

2¾ cups self-rising flour

3 teaspoons ground ginger

2 teaspoons ground allspice

1 teaspoon ground cinnamon

Pinch of salt

2 large eggs, beaten

1 teaspoon baking soda, dissolved in 1 tablespoon warm milk

FROSTING

1⅔ cups confectioners' sugar, sifted

2 pieces of preserved ginger in syrup, drained and chopped, plus ¼ cup preserved ginger syrup

1 tablespoon water (optional)

1. Preheat the oven to 325°F. Grease a 13 x 9-inch baking pan and line it with parchment paper, snipping diagonally into the corners so that the paper fits snugly and allowing the paper to overhang the sides of the pan.

2. In a large, heavy saucepan over low heat, melt the butter, milk, corn syrup, molasses, and sugar. Heat gently until the butter has melted and the sugar dissolved.

3. In a large bowl, mix the flour, spices, and salt, then pour in the warmed milk mixture. Mix until well combined, then add the eggs and dissolved baking soda, and beat until smooth.

4. Pour the mixture into the prepared pan. Bake in the preheated oven for 40–45 minutes, until it has risen—an inserted skewer should come out clean. Carefully lift the paper-lined cake onto a cooling rack, peel away the parchment paper, and let cool completely.

5. To make the frosting, slowly mix the confectioners' sugar with the preserved ginger syrup until thick and smooth, adding the water, if necessary. Pour over the cold gingerbread and spread evenly with a metal spatula.

6. When the frosting is almost set, scatter over the chopped preserved ginger. Let set completely before serving.

VANILLA, HONEY & PEAR CAKE

MAKES ABOUT 16 SQUARES

SPONGE

12 tablespoons (1½ sticks) butter,
    softened, plus extra for greasing
⅔ cup superfine sugar
Seeds scraped from 1 vanilla bean
3 large eggs
1⅔ cups ground hazelnuts
1⅓ cups semolina
2 teaspoons baking powder
3 tablespoons honey
1 teaspoon vanilla extract
15 oz canned pear halves in juice

SYRUP

Seeds scraped from ½ vanilla bean
2 tablespoons honey
1 cup crème fraîche, or ½ cup each
    sour cream and whipping cream
    mixed together, to serve

1. Preheat the oven to 350°F. Grease a 13 x 9-inch baking pan and line the bottom with parchment paper.

2. For the sponge, in a large bowl, beat together the butter, sugar, and vanilla seeds until pale and creamy. Add the eggs, one at a time, beating well between each addition.

3. Fold in the hazelnuts, semolina, and baking powder, followed by the honey and vanilla extract.

4. Pour evenly into the prepared pan, then drain the pears, reserving the juice, slice them, and arrange over the cake mixture, pushing down slightly. Bake in the preheated oven for 30–35 minutes, until it has risen and is golden. An inserted skewer should come out clean.

5. To make a syrup, in a small pan over low heat, add the vanilla seeds, honey, and 3 tablespoons of the reserved pear juice, heat gently, and let barely simmer for 2 minutes. Let cool completely.

6. Remove the cake pan from the oven, drizzle over the cool syrup, and let the cake cool in the pan.

7. When the cake is cold and has absorbed the honey syrup, cut into squares and serve with a dollop of crème fraîche.

BLACKBERRY & ALMOND SHEET CAKE

MAKES ABOUT 24 SQUARES

SPONGE

Butter for greasing
2½ cups fresh or frozen blackberries
1⅓ cups ground almonds
Seeds scraped from 1 vanilla bean
1 cup rice flour, sifted
1½ teaspoons baking powder
6 eggs
1 cup superfine sugar
⅓ cup whole blanched almonds,
   lightly toasted

FROSTING

1½ cups confectioners' sugar, sifted
Finely grated zest and juice of
   ½ orange

1. Preheat the oven to 350°F. Grease a 13 x 9-inch baking pan and line with parchment paper, snipping diagonally into the corners so that the paper fits snugly and allowing the paper to overhand the sides of the pan.

2. Place half of the blackberries in the small bowl of a food processor and process until smooth.

3. In a bowl, mix the ground almonds with the vanilla seeds, rice flour, and baking powder.

4. In a large bowl, beat the eggs with the superfine sugar for 5–6 minutes, until pale, thick, and glossy. Gently fold in the ground almond mixture, along with the pureed and whole blackberries, until well combined.

5. Pour the mixture into the prepared pan and bake in the preheated oven for about 40 minutes, until it has risen and is golden. An inserted skewer should come out clean. Cover lightly with a sheet of parchment paper or foil if it starts to brown too early.

6. Cool for 5 minutes in the pan and then carefully lift the paper-lined cake onto a cooling rack, peeling back as much of the paper as possible. Let cool completely. Peel away the parchment paper.

7. Mix together the frosting ingredients until thick and smooth, then drizzle over the whole sheet cake. Top with the toasted almonds and let the frosting set before cutting into squares.

LIME SHEET CAKE WITH PASSION FRUIT

The sharpness of the lime contrasts well with the buttery passion fruit frosting in this crumbly textured sheet cake. Alternatively, simply open up a passion fruit and scoop the flesh over the top of the cake just before serving.

MAKES 16–18 SQUARES

SHEET CAKE

18 tablespoons (2¼ sticks) butter,
  plus extra for greasing
Finely grated zest and juice of 2 limes
1⅓ cups ground almonds
¾ cup fine cornmeal
1⅓ cups shredded, dried coconut
1 teaspoon baking powder
1 cup superfine sugar
3 eggs, beaten

PASSION FRUIT BUTTERCREAM

5 tablespoons butter, softened
2 cups confectioners' sugar
4 passion fruit, halved, with the
  fruit scooped out

1. Preheat the oven to 300°F. Grease a 13 x 9-inch baking pan and line the bottom with parchment paper.

2. In a small pan over low heat, melt the butter, then pour in the lime zest and juice and set aside.

3. In a large bowl, combine the ground almonds with the cornmeal, coconut, baking powder, and superfine sugar.

4. Beat the melted butter into the eggs and fold into the dry ingredients until just combined. Pour into the prepared pan and bake in the preheated oven for about 50 minutes, until firm and lightly golden. An inserted skewer should come out clean.

5. When cool enough to handle, turn upside down onto a cooling rack to cool completely. Peel away the parchment paper.

6. In a bowl, beat together the buttercream ingredients and spread over the sheet cake before cutting into squares to serve.

TEA-INFUSED "BREAD CAKE"

This heavy sheet cake is a cross between a fruity bread and a cake.
It is delicious served warm or cold with plenty of butter. Wrapped in foil,
it will keep well for several days.

MAKES ONE 9—INCH SQUARE LOAF

⅓ cup chopped dried pears
⅓ cup chopped dried apple
¼ cup chopped dried figs
¼ cup chopped prunes
¼ cup chopped candied orange peel
½ cup raisins
¼ cup golden raisins
½ cup dried currants
½ cup candied cherries, quartered
Finely grated zest of 1 orange
1¼ cups strong earl grey tea
Butter for greasing, plus extra to
    serve
1 egg, beaten
3½ cups self-rising flour
⅔ cup roughly chopped walnuts
1 cup turbinado sugar

1. In a large bowl, add the pears, apple, figs, prunes, orange peel, raisins, currants, cherries, and orange zest, and pour over the tea. Cover and let stand in a cool place to soak overnight.

2. Preheat the oven to 350°F. Grease a 9-inch square cake pan that is at least 1¼ inches deep, and line the bottom with parchment paper.

3. Use a wooden spoon to stir the egg, flour, walnuts, and sugar into the soaked fruit.

4. Turn the thick mixture into the prepared pan, push down evenly with the back of the spoon, and bake in the preheated oven for about an hour, until firm and golden. An inserted skewer should come out clean.

5. Turn out onto a cooling rack and let cool. Peel away the parchment paper and serve sliced with butter.

SPICED PEAR & CIDER SHEET CAKE

Here is a recipe for a delicious, moist cake with a crisp and flaky topping. If you are able to resist, this sheet cake can be kept for a few days in an airtight container.

MAKES 12–16 SQUARES

½ lb (2 sticks) butter, softened, plus extra for greasing

1 cup packed dark brown sugar

3 eggs

2 cups all-purpose flour

2 teaspoons baking powder

1 teaspoon ground allspice

¼ teaspoon salt

1 cup ground hazelnuts

½ cup rolled oats

Scant 1 cup dry pear cider

2 ripe pears, peeled, cored, and chopped

3 tablespoons turbinado sugar

1. Preheat the oven to 350°F. Grease a 13 x 9-inch baking pan and line with parchment paper, snipping diagonally into the corners to fit snugly and allow the paper to overhang the sides.

2. In a large bowl, cream together the butter and sugar until pale and creamy. Add the eggs, one at a time, beating well between each addition.

3. Fold in the flour, baking powder, allspice, and salt, followed by the hazelnuts, oats, and cider. Stir through the chopped pear and turn into the prepared pan, leveling with a rubber spatula.

4. Sprinkle over the turbinado sugar and bake in the preheated oven for about 40 minutes, until it has risen and is golden, with a crispy top.

5. Let cool for a few minutes in the pan before carefully lifting onto a cooling rack to cool completely, peeling back as much of the paper as possible. When cool, peel away the paper and cut into squares to serve.

TIP

If you can't get hold of pear cider for this sheet cake, use a good-quality apple cider. Your local farmers' market will be a good place to look for these ingredients.

PAPAYA, PEACH & MARZIPAN CAKE

The melting marzipan in this delicious, pink-studded sheet cake creates a moist, slightly fudgy texture. It is delicious on the day it is made, but wrapped carefully it will also keep well for a couple of days.

MAKES ABOUT 16 SQUARES

14 tablespoons (1¾ sticks) butter, softened, plus extra for greasing

½ cup ground almonds

1 cup superfine sugar

2 cups self-rising flour

3 eggs

4 peach halves in juice, drained and pureed

1 teaspoon vanilla extract

5½ oz cold marzipan

Scant ½ cup chopped dried papaya

2–3 tablespoons confectioners' sugar, to dust

TO SERVE

1 fresh papaya, sliced

1 fresh peach, sliced

1. Preheat the oven to 350°F. Grease a 13 x 9-inch baking pan and line the bottom with parchment paper.

2. In a large bowl, beat the butter with the almonds, superfine sugar, flour, eggs, pureed peach, and vanilla extract until smooth.

3. Coarsely grate the cold marzipan, then stir into the mixture with the chopped papaya.

4. Turn the mixture into the prepared pan and bake in the preheated oven for 35–40 minutes until golden and it springs back to the touch.

5. Let cool in the pan, then turn out, peel away the parchment paper, and cut into squares. Serve dusted with confectioners' sugar and topped with slices of fresh papaya and peach.

TOFFEE CAKE WITH BUTTERSCOTCH SAUCE

The title for this incredible-tasting sheet cake says it all—and if you have a sweet tooth, what's not to like? Serve it warm as a dessert with the butterscotch sauce, but as plain sponge for a snack with a cup of coffee or tea.

MAKES ABOUT 15 SQUARES

SPONGE
7 tablespoons butter, softened, plus extra for greasing
1⅓ cups chopped, pitted dates
1 teaspoon baking soda
1 tablespoon molasses
⅔ cup boiling water
¾ cup packed light brown sugar
3 eggs
1⅔ cups wholewheat flour
2 teaspoons baking powder
1 teaspoon ground ginger
Pinch of salt
1 tablespoon granulated sugar

BUTTERSCOTCH SAUCE
⅓ cup packed dark brown sugar
5 tablespoons butter
⅓ cup heavy cream
2 tablespoons maple syrup
Good-quality vanilla ice cream, to serve (optional)

1. Preheat the oven to 350°F. Grease a 13 x 9-inch baking pan and line the bottom with parchment paper.

2. In a small bowl, add the dates with the baking soda and pour over the molasses and boiling water, stirring well to combine. Set aside to cool.

3. In a large bowl, beat together the butter and sugar until pale and creamy. Beat in the eggs one at a time, beating well between each addition, then fold in the flour, baking powder, ginger, and salt.

4. Stir the soaked date mixture into the cake mixture, pour into the prepared pan, and sprinkle over the granulated sugar.

5. Bake in the oven for about 30–35 minutes, until it has risen and is deep golden. An inserted skewer should come out clean.

6. In a small, heavy saucepan over low heat, combine all the butterscotch sauce ingredients and heat gently until the sugar has dissolved. Simmer for 1–2 minutes, remove from the heat, and keep warm.

7. Cool the cake for 5–10 minutes in the pan, then turn out, peel away the parchment paper, and cut into squares. Serve with the warmed butterscotch sauce and a scoop of good vanilla ice cream, if liked.

DATE & APPLE MUESLI SQUARES

The only sugar in this recipe is in the dates—but you wouldn't know it from the taste! This very satisfying recipe is also suitable for diabetics.

MAKES 8 SQUARES

18 pitted dates
Scant ½ cup weak black tea
9 tablespoons (1⅛ sticks) butter, melted, plus extra for greasing
3 cups Swiss-style muesli
1 tart apple, grated

1. In a bowl, add the dates and pour over the tea, then let soak for 30 minutes.

2. Meanwhile, preheat the oven to 350°F. Grease a shallow 9-inch square baking pan and line it with parchment paper.

3. In a separate bowl, mix together the muesli and butter, then add the grated apple.

4. When the dates are soft, puree them in a food processor or mash them with a potato masher. Stir the dates into the muesli mix.

5. Spoon the mixture into the prepared pan and smooth over the top lightly. Bake in the preheated oven for 40 minutes, until just cooked but still moist.

6. Let cool slightly before cutting into 8 squares, then let cool completely in the pan. Remove from the parchment paper and lift out with a metal spatula. Store in an airtight container or wrap individually and freeze for up to 1 month.

NUT-TOPPED FRUITY SHEET CAKE

MAKES ONE 9-INCH CAKE

CAKE

¾ cup stout

Finely grated zest of 1 orange

2 tablespoons molasses

½ lb (2 sticks) butter, plus extra for greasing

¾ cup packed dark brown sugar

2¾ cups mixed raisins, dried currants, and golden raisins

¼ cup chopped candied cherries

Scant ⅓ cup chopped candied lemon and orange peels

Scant ½ cup chopped Brazil nuts

3 eggs

½ teaspoon almond extract

1⅔ cups self-rising flour

1 teaspoon ground allspice

3–4 tablespoons smooth apricot jelly, warmed

Mixed nuts, such as walnut and pecan halves, whole blanched almonds and hazelnuts, and whole Brazil nuts, to cover the top of the cake

1. In a large, heavy saucepan over low heat, pour in the stout and orange zest with the molasses, butter, sugar, and fruits. Warm gently and simmer for 3–4 minutes. Set aside to cool completely and to let the fruit absorb most of the liquid, for several hours or preferably overnight.

2. Preheat the oven to 325°F. Grease a deep 9-inch square cake pan and line it with a double layer of parchment paper.

3. Beat the nuts, eggs, and almond extract into the cold fruit mixture, then add the flour and allspice, and mix until well combined.

4. Turn into the prepared pan, making a slight dip in the center of the cake mix, and bake in the preheated oven for about 1½ hours, until firm and an inserted skewer comes out clean.

5. Let cool in the pan before removing, peeling away the parchment paper, and brushing the top of the cake with 2 tablespoons of the warm jelly. Cover the cake attractively with the mixed nuts, then evenly pour over the remaining jelly to glaze the nuts. Let the jelly cool before serving.

TIP
You can also use candied fruit, available at specialty delicatessens, to decorate the cake. Buy beautiful, whole candied fruits, such as clementines and figs. Wrapped and covered properly, this cake will keep for several weeks.

PISTACHIO, LEMON & HONEY BAKLAVA

Baklava is made from layers of phyllo pastry, nuts, sugar, and spices, and drizzled with syrup. The resulting pastry is wonderfully sticky and sweet.

MAKES ABOUT 30 BAKLAVA

9 tablespoons (1⅛ sticks) butter,
    melted, plus extra for greasing
1½ cups shelled pistachio nuts
1 cup whole blanched almonds
1 teaspoon ground cinnamon
½ teaspoon ground allspice
2 tablespoons superfine sugar
12 phyllo pastry sheets

HONEY SYRUP

Grated zest and juice of 2 lemons
1 cup honey
⅔ cup water

1. Preheat the oven to 350°F. Lightly grease a 12 x 8-inch baking pan and line the bottom with parchment paper.

2. Put the pistachio nuts, almonds, and spices in a food processor and process briefly until the nuts are coarsely ground. Stir in the sugar.

3. Cut the sheets of phyllo pastry in half crosswise so they are about the same size as the pan. Brush 1 sheet with melted butter and press it into the prepared pan. Continue to brush and layer the sheets until half remain.

4. Scatter over the nut mixture and then top with the remaining pastry, brushing each sheet with melted butter as you proceed.

5. Use a sharp knife to score a diamond pattern into the pastry, cutting down to the bottom. Drizzle over any remaining butter and bake in the preheated oven for 20 minutes.

6. Reduce the oven temperature to 325°F and bake for 20–25 minutes more, until the pastry is crisp and golden.

7. Meanwhile, make the syrup. In a saucepan over low-medium heat, add the lemon zest, lemon juice, honey, and water and heat gently until boiling. Simmer for 5 minutes, then pour the hot syrup over the baklava and let cool in the pan.

MAPLE-FROSTED PECAN SHEET CAKE

This soft, pecan sponge cake, topped with a mound of snowy white, maple-infused frosting, is impressive enough for any occasion.

MAKES ABOUT 16 SLICES

SPONGE

12 tablespoons (1½ sticks) butter, softened, plus extra for greasing

1¼ cup pecans

1½ cups self-rising flour

1½ teaspoons baking powder

¼ teaspoon ground nutmeg

Generous ¾ cup superfine sugar

3 eggs

1 teaspoon vanilla extract

3 tablespoons milk

FROSTING

Generous ¾ cup superfine sugar

1 egg white

2 tablespoons water

¼ teaspoon cream of tartar

Pinch of salt

2 tablespoons maple syrup

1¼ cups pecan halves, to decorate

1. Preheat the oven to 350°F. Grease a 13 x 9-inch baking pan and line the bottom with parchment paper.

2. In a small skillet, gently dry-fry the pecans until toasted. Turn into a heatproof bowl to cool, then finely chop them.

3. In a large bowl, mix the chopped nuts with the flour, baking powder, ground nutmeg, and sugar. Add the butter, eggs, vanilla extract, and milk, and beat well for 2–3 minutes.

4. Turn the mixture into the prepared pan and bake in the preheated oven for 25–30 minutes, until it has risen, is springy, and inserted skewer comes out clean. Turn out onto a cooling rack, peel away the parchment paper, and let cool completely.

5. To make the frosting, in a large heatproof bowl set over a saucepan of gently simmering water, heat the sugar, egg whites, water, cream of tartar, salt, and maple syrup, stirring until the sugar has dissolved. Beat with an electric beater until the mixture is stiff and stands up in soft peaks. This will take 8–10 minutes. Remove from the heat.

6. Place the cooled cake on a serving plate, spread with the frosting, and decorate with the pecan halves before cutting into slices to serve.

JAMMY ALMOND SPONGE CAKE

Use your preferred jam in this almond pastry sheet cake. This would be perfect for cutting into slices and selling at your next cake sale.

MAKES ABOUT 20 SQUARES

½ lb (2 sticks) butter, softened, plus extra for greasing
8-oz package prepared pie dough
Scant ½ cup all-purpose flour, plus extra for dusting
½ cup jam, such as raspberry
1 cup superfine sugar
4 eggs
1½ cups ground almonds
1 cup slivered almonds, lightly toasted

1. Preheat the oven to 350°F. Lightly grease a 13 x 9-inch baking pan.

2. Roll out the pie dough on a lightly floured surface and lift into the prepared pan so that it covers the bottom and comes up the sides, overhanging slightly. Cover the bottom with an even layer of jam.

3. In a large bowl, beat together the butter and sugar until pale and creamy. Add the eggs, one at a time, beating well and adding a spoonful of almonds between each addition. Fold in the remaining ground almonds and flour, then dollop spoonfuls over the jam layer, spreading them evenly with the back of the spoon.

4. Sprinkle over the slivered almonds and bake in the preheated oven for about 35 minutes, until firm and golden. Trim the pastry.

5. Let cool slightly in the pan before cutting into squares and lifting with a metal spatula onto a cooling rack to cool completely.

WHOLEWHEAT CAKE WITH ZUCCHINI

Here is a healthier alternative to most sheet cakes, with canola oil replacing the butter and yogurt, and zucchini providing the moist texture. The cream cheese frosting is provided as entirely optional, but it is very delicious!

MAKES 16 SQUARES

SPONGE
1 cup canola or sunflower oil, plus extra for greasing
2⅓ cups wholewheat flour
2 teaspoons baking powder
½ teaspoon salt
1½ teaspoons baking soda
1 large zucchini (about 14 oz), coarsely grated
3 eggs
1 cup packed light brown sugar
scant ½ cup honey
½ cup plain yogurt
⅔ cup golden raisins

CREAM CHEESE FROSTING (OPTIONAL)
2 tablespoons butter, softened
½ cup cream cheese
¾ cup confectioners' sugar
Juice and finely grated zest of 1 lime

1. Preheat the oven to 350°F. Grease a 9-inch square cake pan and line it with parchment paper, snipping diagonally into the corners so it fits snugly over the bottom and up the sides of the pan.

2. In a medium bowl, mix the flour with the baking powder, salt, and baking soda. Squeeze the grated zucchini to remove excess water and stir into the flour mix.

3. In a separate large bowl, beat the eggs with the sugar for 6–7 minutes, until pale and creamy. Slowly beat in the honey, oil, and yogurt, and then fold in the flour-and-zucchini mixture along with the golden raisins.

4. Pour into the prepared pan and bake in the preheated oven for about 55 minutes, until firm. An inserted skewer should come out clean. Let cool completely in the pan.

5. Turn the cake onto a serving plate and peel away the parchment paper. If liked, beat together the butter, cream cheese, confectioners' sugar, and lime juice until smooth, then spread over the top of the cake. Sprinkle with lime zest and cut into squares to serve.

SPICED APPLE, DATE & HAZELNUT CAKE

If you are looking for a good lighter alternative to a heavy, traditional fruit cake, then this is it. The apples and spices will fill your kitchen with wonderful aromas.

MAKES 16 SLICES

12 tablespoons (1½ sticks) butter, softened, plus extra for greasing
⅓ cup whole blanched hazelnuts
¾ cup packed light brown sugar
1½ cups self-rising flour
½ teaspoon ground cinnamon
Pinch of salt
3 eggs, lightly beaten
½ cup unsweetened applesauce
1 teaspoon freshly grated ginger root
15 soft dried dates, pitted and chopped
2 apples, peeled, cored, and diced
25 brown sugar cubes (about 1¾ oz), roughly crushed

1. Preheat the oven to 350°F. Grease a 9-inch square cake pan and line the bottom with parchment paper.

2. In a small skillet over low-medium heat, gently dry-fry the hazelnuts until lightly golden, shaking the skillet frequently so they don't burn. Cool slightly, then tap lightly with a rolling pin to break up a little.

3. In a large bowl, beat together the butter and sugar until pale and creamy. Sift in the flour, cinnamon, and salt, then add the eggs, applesauce, and ginger root and fold gently until combined. Stir in half the dates and half the chopped apple.

4. Use a rubber spatula to turn the mixture into the prepared pan, then scatter the top with the remaining chopped dates and apple, the toasted hazelnuts, and the crushed sugar cubes.

5. Bake in the preheated oven for about 45 minutes, until firm and golden. An inserted skewer should come out clean.

6. Let cool in the pan for a few minutes, then turn out onto a cooling rack to cool completely. Peel away the parchment paper, and cut into slices to serve.

WALNUT & PUMPKIN CAKE WITH SYRUP

Similar to a steamed syrup sponge, this walnut and pumpkin sheet cake is baked with a syrup that settles in the bottom of the cake. When turned out onto a serving dish, the syrup forms a sticky topping that is delicious served warm.

MAKES 12–16 SQUARES

½ lb (2 sticks) butter, softened, plus extra for greasing

Generous ⅓ cup dark corn syrup, plus ¼ cup, warmed slightly, to serve (optional)

¾ cup superfine sugar

3 eggs

Generous ⅓ cup sweet pumpkin puree

1¾ cups self-rising flour

1 teaspoon baking powder

1⅔ cups finely chopped walnuts

1. Preheat the oven to 350°F. Grease a 9-inch square cake pan.

2. Pour the dark corn syrup over the bottom of the prepared pan.

3. In a large bowl, beat together the butter and sugar until pale and creamy. Add the eggs, one at a time, beating well between each addition.

4. Fold in the pumpkin puree with the flour, baking powder, and walnuts, and pour over the syrup layer, smoothing with a rubber spatula.

5. Bake in the preheated oven for about 30 minutes, until firm and golden.

6. Let cool for a few minutes before turning onto a serving plate, syrup side up. Serve warm or cold with a drizzle of warm syrup, if liked.

CORNMEAL & FRUIT SHEET CAKE

Here is a wonderful sheet cake that is equally suitable served cold on a summer's day with a dollop of crème fraîche, or warm on a winter's evening.

MAKES 12–16 SQUARES

SPONGE

½ cup vegetable oil, plus extra for greasing

1 lb frozen mixed fruit, such as strawberries, raspberries, and blackberries

1 cup superfine sugar

3 eggs

1 cup Greek yogurt

Finely grated zest of 1 orange

Generous ¾ cup ground almonds

1 teaspoon baking powder

1 cup instant cornmeal

2 teaspoons poppy seeds

SYRUP

Scant 1 cup orange juice

¾ cup superfine sugar

1. Preheat the oven to 350°F. Grease a 9-inch square cake pan, then mix the mixed fruit with half the sugar and pack over the bottom of the pan.

2. To make the syrup, in a small, heavy saucepan over low heat, add the orange juice and sugar, and heat gently until the sugar has dissolved. Increase the heat slightly and simmer for 5–6 minutes to create a thin syrup. Set aside to cool.

3. In a medium bowl, beat the vegetable oil with the eggs, Greek yogurt, and orange zest.

4. In a separate large bowl, mix the ground almonds, baking powder, cornmeal, and poppy seeds, then make a well in the center. Pour in the vegetable oil mixture and beat to create a smooth batter.

5. Pour the batter over the mixed fruit and bake in the preheated oven for 40–45 minutes, until it has risen and is golden and firm to the touch.

6. Remove the cake from the oven and prick all over using the tines of a fork. Pour over ½ cup of the cooled syrup and let the cake stand to cool and absorb the syrup in the pan.

7. Turn onto a large serving plate, cut into squares, and serve drizzled with the remaining syrup.

HONEY & SPICE SHEET CAKE

These delicious squares have sugar and spice and everything nice, and the honey adds just the right amount of sweetness to make them irresistible.

MAKES 24 SQUARES

2 cups honey
½ cup oil, plus extra for greasing
1¼ cups superfine sugar
6 cups all-purpose flour
1 tablespoon baking powder
2⅔ cups ground almonds
2 teaspoons ground cinnamon
½ teaspoon ground allspice
Pinch of ground cloves
Pinch of salt
3 eggs
1 cup chopped, mixed candied peel
2 tablespoons evaporated milk

TO DECORATE

Almond halves
Candied cherries
Candied lemon peel

1. In a medium, heavy saucepan over low-medium heat, bring the honey to a boil with the oil and sugar, stirring continuously, until the sugar has dissolved. Let cool.

2. In a large bowl, sift the flour with the baking powder and mix with the ground almonds, spices, salt, eggs, and mixed peel. Add the cooled honey mixture and knead well. If the dough is too soft, add a little more flour. Cover and let rest for 1 hour in the refrigerator.

3. Preheat the oven to 375°F. Grease two 13 x 9-inch jelly roll pans and line with parchment paper, snipping diagonally into the corners to fit snugly and allowing the paper to overhang the sides of the pan.

4. With floured hands, press the dough into the prepared pans, smooth the surface, and brush with the evaporated milk. Lightly cut 2¾-inch squares in the mixture with a sharp knife.

5. Decorate each square with almonds, cherries, and pieces of candied lemon peel. Bake in the center of the preheated oven for 25–30 minutes.

6. Let cool slightly, then carefully lift the paper-lined cakes out onto a cooling rack. Let cool completely. Peel away the parchment paper and cut into squares.

UPSIDE-DOWN BANANA SHEET CAKE

This sweet banana cake is great served cold as a delicious moist cake and even better still warm with a scoop of good-quality vanilla ice cream.

MAKES 12–16 SQUARES

23 tablespoons (2⅞ sticks) butter, softened, plus extra for greasing
5 small ripe bananas (about 14 oz peeled)
1¼ cups packed light brown sugar
2 eggs
1¾ cups self-rising flour
1 teaspoon baking soda
½ cup chopped dried banana
⅓ cup chopped prunes
3 tablespoons milk

1. Preheat the oven to 350°F. Grease a 9-inch square cake pan. Slice 3 of the bananas into ¼-inch thick slices and arrange over the bottom of the prepared pan.

2. In a small, heavy saucepan over low heat, melt 7 tablespoons of the butter with ⅓ cup of the sugar, stirring until syrupy. Pour over the banana slices, then set aside.

3. In a large bowl, beat together the remaining butter and sugar until pale and creamy, then add the eggs, one at a time, beating well between each addition.

4. In a small bowl, mash the remaining bananas with a fork.

5. Fold the flour and baking soda into the butter mixture, followed by the mashed bananas, dried banana, prunes, and milk.

6. Spoon the mixture over the sliced bananas in the pan and level with the back of the spoon. Bake in the preheated oven for 40–45 minutes, until it has risen and is golden. An inserted skewer should come out clean.

7. Let cool in the pan for 5–10 minutes, then turn out onto a cooling rack, being careful because some hot syrup may trickle out. Serve cut into squares, warm or cold.

CRUMBLY CHERRY & ALMOND SLICES

MAKES 12–16 SLICES

CAKE BASE

11 tablespoons (1⅜ sticks) butter, softened, plus extra for greasing

1⅓ cups ground almonds

1½ cups all-purpose flour

Seeds scraped from 1 vanilla bean

⅓ cup superfine sugar

Finely grated zest of 1 lemon

2 large egg yolks

¾ cup good-quality cherry jelly or sweet compote

CRUMBLE TOPPING

1½ cups all-purpose flour

⅓ cup granulated sugar

Chopped almonds, lightly toasted

7 tablespoons butter, melted

2–3 tablespoons confectioners' sugar, to dust

1. Preheat the oven to 375°F. Grease an 11 x 7-inch baking pan.

2. In a large bowl, mix the ground almonds with the flour, vanilla seeds, superfine sugar, and lemon zest. Add the butter and egg yolks, and mix to a dough with your hands.

3. Place the dough in the prepared pan and push with your knuckles to cover the bottom evenly. Cover lightly with plastic wrap and let rest in the refrigerator for 20 minutes.

4. For the crumble, place the flour, sugar, and chopped almonds in a medium bowl, and mix in the melted butter until lumpy.

5. Spread the cherry jelly or compote over the cake base, sprinkle over the crumble topping, and bake in the preheated oven for about 35 minutes, until crispy and lightly golden, and the jelly is bubbling.

6. Let cool in the pan before cutting into slices and lifting out with a metal spatula. Serve dusted with confectioners' sugar.

TIP
These crumble slices can be frozen. Just remove from the freezer and reheat in a low oven until warm. Serve with a drizzle of heavy cream as a great, low-effort dessert.

FROSTED CARROT & POPPY SEED CAKE

MAKES 12–16 SQUARES

CARROT CAKE
1 cup sunflower oil, plus extra
    for greasing
4 eggs
1 cup superfine sugar
1 tablespoon molasses
2 cups wholewheat flour
1 tablespoon baking powder
½ teaspoon salt
1 teaspoon baking soda
2 tablespoons poppy seeds
6 large organic carrots (about 1 lb),
    washed and coarsely grated
⅔ cup roughly chopped walnuts

FROSTING
1¼ cups cream cheese
3½ tablespoons butter, softened
½ teaspoon vanilla extract
1 teaspoon lemon juice
1 cup confectioners' sugar
⅔ cup walnut halves, to decorate
    (optional)

1. Preheat the oven to 325°F. Grease a 9-inch square cake pan and line it with parchment paper, snipping diagonally into the corners so it fits snugly over the bottom and up the sides.

2. In a large bowl, beat together the eggs, sugar, and molasses until pale and thick.

3. Sift in the flour, baking powder, salt, and baking soda, and fold in well. Add the poppy seeds, carrots, and walnuts, then pour over the oil, and stir until well combined.

4. Turn into the prepared pan and bake in the preheated oven for about 1 hour, until it has risen, is golden, and an inserted skewer comes out clean.

5. Let cool in the pan for 10 minutes before turning out, upside down, onto a cooling rack to cool completely. Peel away the parchment paper.

6. To make the frosting, in a medium bowl, beat together the cream cheese, butter, vanilla extract, lemon juice, and confectioners' sugar until thick and smooth.

7. Spread the frosting over the top and sides of the cake, covering it completely. Decorate with the walnut halves and cut into squares to serve.

COCONUT & PINEAPPLE SHEET CAKE

Bring a taste of the Tropics to your kitchen with this coconut and pineapple cake. Using fresh pineapple and crème fraîche provides a delicious moist sponge cake that contrasts with the crisp crumble topping.

MAKES 12–16 SQUARES

CRUMBLE
¼ cup all-purpose flour

½ cup packed dark brown sugar

2 tablespoons shredded, dried coconut

3½ tablespoons butter, softened

SPONGE
9 tablespoons (1⅛ sticks) butter, plus extra for greasing

1 cup superfine sugar

3 eggs

1⅔ cups all-purpose flour

2 teaspoons baking powder

¼ teaspoon salt

⅔ cup crème fraîche, or ⅓ cup sour cream mixed with ⅓ cup whipping cream

⅓ cup shredded, dried coconut

1 cup fresh or canned pineapple chunks

1. Preheat the oven to 350°F. Grease a deep, 9-inch square cake pan and line it with parchment paper, snipping diagonally into the corners so it fits snugly over the bottom and up the sides of the pan.

2. For the crumble topping, mix together the flour, brown sugar, and dried coconut in a bowl, and rub in the butter until the mixture is lumpy. Set aside.

3. To make the cake, in a large bowl, beat together the butter and sugar until pale and creamy. Add the eggs, one at a time, beating well between each addition.

4. Fold in the flour, baking powder, and salt, followed by the crème fraîche and dried coconut.

5. Turn the mixture into the prepared pan and then scatter over the pineapple chunks and crumble topping. Bake in the preheated oven for about 1 hour and 20 minutes, until firm and golden. An inserted skewer should come out clean.

6. Let cool in the pan, then carefully lift out, peel away the parchment paper, and cut into squares. Serve slightly warm or cool.

MUFFINS & CUPCAKES

BLUEBERRY & POPPY SEED MUFFINS

The blueberries in this recipe lend the muffins a wonderful moist texture. The ricotta and vanilla give them a creamy richness, which is a perfect backdrop for the tiny black poppy seeds.

MAKES 6 MUFFINS
(double quantities for 12)

5 tablespoons butter, softened, plus extra for greasing (if needed)
½ cup ricotta cheese
⅓ cup superfine sugar
Seeds scraped from ½ vanilla bean
1 large egg, lightly beaten
1¼ cups all-purpose flour
1½ teaspoons baking powder
Pinch of salt
Scant ½ cup milk
1 tablespoon poppy seeds
½ cup fresh or frozen blueberries

1. Preheat the oven to 350°F. Line a muffin pan with 6 paper muffin liners. Alternatively, grease 6 cups in a nonstick or silicone muffin pan with butter.

2. In a large bowl, beat the butter with the ricotta, sugar, and vanilla seeds until pale and creamy. Add the egg and beat well.

3. Sift the flour, baking powder, and salt into the butter mixture and pour over the milk. Fold gently until the ingredients are just combined, then stir in the poppy seeds and blueberries.

4. Spoon the mixture into the paper liners or prepared cups, and bake in the preheated oven for about 35 minutes, until they have risen and are firm to touch.

5. Remove the muffins from the pan and cool on a cooling rack.

OAT BRAN & BANANA MUFFINS

These muffins are full of fruit and perfect for a healthy, satisfying breakfast. Top with strawberry or banana, or leave plain for the "au naturel" look.

MAKES 6 MUFFINS
(double quantities for 12)

2 tablespoons butter, melted, plus extra for greasing (if needed)
⅓ cup raisins
⅓ cup packed dark brown sugar
¾ cup wholewheat flour
1 teaspoon baking powder
¼ teaspoon salt
½ cup oat bran
1 egg, lightly beaten
2 tablespoons honey
½ cup buttermilk
1 teaspoon vanilla extract
1 small, ripe banana, mashed
1 small carrot, grated
3 tablespoons applesauce
6 dried strawberries or crisp banana chips, to decorate (optional)

1. Preheat the oven to 350°F. Line a muffin pan with 6 paper muffin liners. Alternatively, grease 6 cups in a nonstick or silicone muffin pan with butter.

2. In a large bowl, mix the raisins with the sugar, flour, baking powder, salt, and oat bran.

3. In a separate bowl, beat the egg with the honey, melted butter, buttermilk, and vanilla extract. Pour into the dry ingredients and add the mashed banana, grated carrot, and applesauce. Fold gently until the ingredients are barely combined.

4. Spoon the mixture into the paper liners or prepared cups, top with a dried strawberry or banana chip, if using, and bake in the preheated oven for about 30 minutes, until they have risen and are firm to touch.

5. Remove the muffins from the pan and cool on a cooling rack.

CRUNCHY CINNAMON APPLE MUFFINS

These moist, cinnamon-flavored muffins have a crunchy topping. They are filling, but not too sweet, making them the perfect choice for brunch or an afternoon snack.

MAKES 6 MUFFINS
(double quantities for 12)

2 tablespoons butter, plus extra fro greasing (if needed)
2 teaspoons honey
1 cup all-purpose flour
⅓ cup packed dark brown sugar
¾ teaspoon baking powder
¾ teaspoon ground cinnamon
1 small apple, such as Granny Smith, peeled and coarsely grated
⅓ cup milk
⅓ cup vegetable oil
1 egg, lightly beaten

TOPPING
2 tablespoons turbinado sugar
Pinch of ground cinnamon

1. Preheat the oven to 350°F. Line a muffin pan with 6 paper muffin liners. Alternatively, grease 6 cups in a nonstick or silicone muffin pan with butter.

2. In a small saucepan over low heat, melt the butter with the honey.

3. To make the sugar topping, in a small bowl, mix the turbinado sugar with the pinch of cinnamon, then set aside.

4. In a large bowl, mix the flour with the dark brown sugar, baking powder, and cinnamon, then stir in the grated apple. Gently fold the milk, oil, and egg into the dry ingredients along with the melted butter and honey until just combined.

5. Spoon the mixture into the paper liners or prepared cups, sprinkle with the sugar topping, and bake in the preheated oven for 30 minutes, until the muffins have risen and are golden.

6. Cool the muffins on a cooling rack.

HONEY, OAT & YOGURT MUFFINS

These oaty muffins are ideal made for breakfast or a mid-morning snack.

They are easy to make—as long as you don't overmix the mixture.

MAKES 6 MUFFINS
(double quantities for 12)

2 tablespoons butter, melted, plus
   extra for greasing (if needed)
½ cup honey
Scant ½ cup Greek yogurt
2 tablespoons milk
2 tablespoons vegetable oil
1 egg, lightly beaten
Generous ½ cup rolled oats, plus
   1 tablespoon
¾ cup all-purpose flour
1 teaspoon baking powder
¼ teaspoon baking soda
Pinch of salt

1. Preheat the oven to 350°F. Line a muffin pan with 6 paper muffin liners. Alternatively, grease 6 cups in a nonstick or silicone muffin pan with butter.

2. In a small bowl, beat together the melted butter, honey, Greek yogurt, milk, oil, and egg.

3. In a large bowl, mix all but the 1 tablespoon rolled oats with the flour, baking powder, baking soda, and salt. Gently fold the wet ingredients into the dry ingredients until just combined.

4. Spoon the muffin mixture into the paper liners or prepared cups and sprinkle with the extra tablespoon of oats. Bake in the preheated oven for 25–30 minutes, until they have risen and are firm to touch.

5. Remove the muffins from the pan and cool on a cooling rack.

PUMPKIN MUFFINS WITH MAPLE DRIZZLE

These delicious muffins are great served at any time of the day, warm or cold, with or without the maple drizzle, so they should be perfect for whatever your craving!

MAKES 6 MUFFINS
(double quantities for 12)

Butter for greasing (if needed)
1 cup wholewheat flour
1 teaspoon baking powder
½ teaspoon baking soda
½ teaspoon ground ginger
½ teaspoon ground allspice
Pinch of salt
⅓ cup sunflower oil
⅓ cup crème fraîche, or
   2½ tablespoons sour cream
   mixed with 2½ tablespoons
   whipping cream
3 tablespoons maple syrup
1 egg, lightly beaten
⅓ cup packed light brown sugar
⅔ cup grated pumpkin flesh
3 tablespoons sunflower seeds

1. Preheat the oven to 350°F. Line a muffin pan with 6 paper muffin liners. Alternatively, grease 6 cups in a nonstick or silicone muffin pan with butter.

2. In a large bowl, mix together the flour, baking powder, baking soda, spices, and salt.

3. In a separate bowl, beat together the oil, crème fraîche, 1 tablespoon of the maple syrup, and the egg with the sugar. Pour the wet ingredients into the dry ingredients and gently fold in until just combined.

4. Add the grated pumpkin and 2 tablespoons of sunflower seeds, and stir gently.

5. Spoon the mixture into the paper liners or prepared cups, scatter over the remaining seeds, and bake in the preheated oven for 20–25 minutes, until they have risen and are firm.

6. Remove the muffins from the pan and cool on a cooling rack. Warm the remaining maple syrup slightly and drizzle over the muffins.

PEANUT BUTTER & CHOCOLATE MUFFINS

These crunchy muffins with a melting chocolate center have a delicious salty sweetness, making them perfect for any moment of the day.

MAKES 6 MUFFINS
(double quantities for 12)

2 tablespoons butter, plus extra for greasing (if needed)
Generous ⅓ cup chunky peanut butter
1¼ cups all-purpose flour
2 teaspoons baking powder
¼ cup superfine sugar
Pinch of salt
1 egg, lightly beaten
Scant ½ cup milk
6 chunks of milk chocolate

1. Preheat the oven to 350°F. Line a muffin pan with 6 paper muffin liners. Alternatively, grease 6 cups in a nonstick or silicone muffin pan with butter.

2. In a small saucepan over low heat, melt the butter with the peanut butter, then set aside.

3. In a large bowl, stir together the flour, baking powder, sugar, and salt. Add the egg, milk, and melted butter mixture, and gently fold the ingredients until just combined.

4. Spoon the mixture into the paper liners or prepared cups, then push a chunk of chocolate into the center of each one. Bake in the preheated oven for 20–25 minutes, until they have risen and are golden.

5. Remove the muffins from the pan and cool on a cooling rack.

TIP
These muffins are best served slightly warm, but they will keep for 48 hours in an airtight container.

TOFFEE APPLE MUFFIN

This huge "muffin" is a great standby that few people can resist. During cooking, the sugar melts to form a deliciously smooth, toffee-like sauce for the apples. It is perfect served with homemade vanilla ice cream.

SERVES 4

3 apples, peeled, cored, and thickly
   sliced
¾ cup self-rising flour, plus
   1 tablespoon
½ cup packed light brown sugar
¼ cup superfine sugar
½ teaspoon ground allspice
1 egg, lightly beaten
½ cup plain yogurt
4 tablespoons butter, melted

1. Preheat the oven to 425°F.

2. In a shallow, heatproof dish, toss the apples with the 1 tablespoon of flour and the brown sugar.

3. In a large bowl, mix the remaining flour with the superfine sugar and allspice. Add the egg, yogurt, and butter, and gently fold until the ingredients are just combined.

4. Spoon the mixture over the apples and bake in the preheated oven for 15–20 minutes, until just firm and golden.

5. Remove the muffins from the pan and let cool slightly on a cooling rack before serving warm.

RHUBARB MUFFINS WITH ROSE CREAM

MAKES 6 MUFFINS
(double quantities for 12)

ROSE-WATER CREAM

⅔ cup heavy cream

1 teaspoon rose water

3 tablespoons confectioners' sugar, sifted

CRUMBLE TOPPING

1 tablespoon butter, softened

2 tablespoons all-purpose flour

1 tablespoon ground almonds

Pinch of salt

1 tablespoon turbinado sugar

MUFFINS

¾ cup fresh or frozen sliced rhubarb

Finely grated zest and juice of
    ½ orange

½ cup packed light brown sugar

1 cup all-purpose flour

1 teaspoon baking powder

½ teaspoon baking soda

1 egg, lightly beaten

2 tablespoons butter, melted

Scant ½ cup buttermilk

1–2 tablespoons orange juice

1. Preheat the oven to 350°F. Line a muffin pan with 6 paper muffin liners.

2. To make the rose-water cream, in a small bowl, beat the cream with the rose water and confectioners' sugar until smooth. Cover and place in the refrigerator.

3. To make the crumble topping, in a small bowl, rub the butter into the flour using your fingertips. Stir in the ground almonds, salt, and sugar and rub until it turns lumpy. Set aside.

4. In a small saucepan over low heat, gently heat the rhubarb, orange juice, and brown sugar until the sugar has dissolved and the fruit softens. Set aside to cool.

5. In a large bowl, mix the orange zest with the flour, baking powder, and baking soda in a large bowl. In a separate small bowl, beat the egg with the melted butter, buttermilk, and orange juice. Pour the beaten egg mixture into the dry ingredients along with the cooled, syrupy rhubarb and gently fold the ingredients until just combined.

6. Spoon the mixture into the paper liners, sprinkle a little crumble topping over each one, and bake in the preheated oven for about 30 minutes, until they have risen and are golden brown.

7. Remove the muffins from the pan and cool on a cooling rack. Serve with the rose-water cream.

CRANBERRY & ORANGE MUFFINS

The combination of the orange-scented cake with the soft, slightly tart flavor of dried cranberry, make these an ideal brunch addition.

MAKES 12 MUFFINS

5 tablespoons butter, melted, plus
   extra for greasing (if needed)
¾ cup milk
1 egg, lightly beaten
Finely grated zest of 1 orange
1 teaspoon vanilla extract
2½ cups self-rising flour
2 teaspoons baking powder
⅔ cup dried cranberries
¼ cup vanilla sugar
¼ cup packed light brown sugar

1. Preheat the oven to 375°F. Line a muffin pan with 12 paper muffin liners. Alternatively, grease 12 cups in a nonstick or silicone muffin pan with butter.

2. In a small bowl, mix together the butter, milk, egg, orange zest, and vanilla extract.

3. In a large bowl, sift the flour and baking powder together and stir in the cranberries and the sugars.

4. Add the milk mixture to the dry ingredients and gently fold until the ingredients are just combined.

5. Spoon the mixture into the paper liners or prepared cups, piling it up in the center. Bake the muffins in the preheated oven for 15–20 minutes until they have risen and are golden brown.

6. Remove the muffins from the pan and let cool slightly on a cooling rack before serving warm.

TIP
Dried blueberries or cherries are equally good alternatives to the cranberries. You can also omit the orange zest and use a teaspoon of ground cinnamon or allspice instead.

MARBLED MASCARPONE MUFFINS

The contrast of creamy pale mascarpone swirled with the rich dark chocolate makes these irresistible muffins look impressive—and they taste just as delicious as they look.

MAKES 6 MUFFINS
(double quantities for 12)

2 tablespoons butter, melted, plus extra for greasing (if needed)
¾ cup all-purpose flour
2 teaspoons baking powder
¼ cup superfine sugar
¼ teaspoon salt
½ cup mascarpone cheese
1 egg
3 tablespoons milk
½ teaspoon vanilla extract
3½ oz dark chocolate, melted
1 tablespoon unsweetened cocoa
¼ cup dark chocolate chips

1. Preheat the oven to 350°F. Line a muffin pan with 6 paper muffin liners. Alternatively, grease 6 cups in a nonstick or silicone muffin pan with butter.

2. In a large bowl, mix the flour with the baking powder, sugar, and salt.

3. In a small bowl, add the mascarpone with the melted butter, egg, milk, and vanilla extract and beat until smooth.

4. Gently fold the wet ingredients into the dry ingredients until just combined, then turn a third of this mix into a small bowl. Add the melted chocolate and unsweetened cocoa to the remaining mixture in the large bowl and gently fold in until just combined.

5. Gently fold the chocolate chips into the white mixture until just combined. Fill the paper liners or prepared cups halfway with the dark chocolate mix, spoon over the white batter, and then top with the remaining dark chocolate mixture.

6. Use a teaspoon to swirl the two mixtures slightly, then bake in the preheated oven for 25–30 minutes, until they have risen and are firm to touch.

7. Remove the muffins from the pan and cool on a cooling rack.

RED VELVET CUPCAKES

The vast amount of red food dye normally used in a red velvet recipe is replaced here by a natural alternative. Pureed beet give these cupcakes a darker, more low-key, rusty-red sheen—and the taste is infinitely better!

MAKES 12 CUPCAKES

CUPCAKES

1¾ cups cooked sliced beets

½ cup unsweetened applesauce

1½ teaspoons vanilla extract

1¾ oz dark chocolate, melted and cooled

2 eggs, lightly beaten

½ cup vegetable oil

1 cup superfine sugar

1¼ cups all-purpose flour

1½ teaspoons baking soda

½ teaspoon baking powder

½ teaspoon salt

3 tablespoons dark chocolate chips

FROSTING

⅔ cup cream cheese

5 tablespoons butter, softened

Generous ⅓ cup confectioners' sugar, sifted

2–3 drops vanilla extract

1 teaspoon lemon juice

2–3 tablespoons fresh coconut shavings, to decorate (optional)

1. Preheat the oven to 350°F. Line a cupcake pan with 12 paper cupcake liners.

2. In a food processor, process the beets with the applesauce and vanilla extract until smooth.

3. Turn the puree into a large bowl and add the melted chocolate, eggs, vegetable oil, and sugar. Beat well for 2–3 minutes.

4. Sift in the flour, baking soda, baking powder, and salt, and fold until smooth. Lightly fold in the chocolate chips, then spoon the mixture into the paper liners.

5. Bake in the preheated oven for about 35 minutes, until they are risen and firm to touch. Let cool for 4–5 minutes before transferring to a cooling rack to cool completely.

6. To make the frosting, in a medium bowl, beat together the cream cheese, butter, confectioners' sugar, vanilla extract, and lemon juice until really smooth, then spread or pipe over the cupcakes. Decorate with the coconut, if liked, and serve.

TIP

If using fresh beets, choose the reddest variety possible and boil until just soft, because overcooking will also leech color out of the beets.

ROCKY FRUIT 'N' NUT CUPCAKES

Strictly speaking, this cupcake is not really a cupcake but a cross between a cookie and a rock cake. It has a heavy, crumbly texture full of fruit and is topped with almonds and cherries.

MAKES 12 CUPCAKES

CUPCAKES
¼ lb (1 stick) cold butter, plus extra for greasing
2 cups all-purpose flour
½ teaspoon ground cinnamon
Pinch of ground nutmeg
¼ teaspoon salt
1 teaspoon baking powder
⅓ cup superfine sugar
Finely grated zest of 1 orange
Finely grated zest of 1 lemon
½ cup dried currants
⅓ cup raisins
1 egg, lightly beaten
3–4 tablespoons milk

EGG WASH
1 egg yolk
1 tablespoon water
Pinch of salt

TO DECORATE
6 candied cherries, halved
12 whole blanched almonds

1. Preheat the oven to 400°F. Lightly grease 12 cups in a nonstick or silicone cupcake pan with butter.

2. In a large bowl, add the flour, cinnamon, nutmeg, salt, and baking powder, and rub in the butter until it resembles fine bread crumbs.

3. Stir in the sugar, orange zest, lemon zest, currants, and raisins.

4. Add the beaten egg and milk, and mix to form a soft dough. Divide the dough into 12 rough balls and drop each one into a prepared cup.

5. Make an egg wash by beating the egg yolk, water, and salt in a small dish. Brush the egg wash over the cakes, then push half a cherry and an almond onto each one.

6. Bake in the preheated oven for 15–20 minutes, until golden and firm to touch. Transfer to a cooling rack to cool a little and serve warm.

COCONUT SNOWBALL FROSTED CUPCAKES

Get ready for a coconut explosion from these gorgeous, fluffy cupcakes. Try making them in shiny, silver liners, which look great against the white flakes of coconut.

MAKES 12 CUPCAKES

CUPCAKES

1⅔ cups self-rising flour
⅔ cup superfine sugar
½ cup shredded, dried coconut
½ teaspoon salt
¾ cup coconut milk
½ cup vegetable oil
2 eggs, lightly beaten

FROSTING

⅔ cup cream cheese
2 tablespoons butter
Generous ⅓ cup confectioners' sugar
½ teaspoon vanilla extract
2 tablespoons shredded coconut

1. Preheat the oven to 350°F. Line a cupcake pan with 12 paper cupcake liners.

2. In a large bowl, mix together the self-rising flour, sugar, shredded coconut, and salt. Make a well in the center and add the coconut milk, vegetable oil, and eggs. Beat well until the mixture is smooth.

3. Spoon the mixture into the paper liners and bake in the preheated oven for about 20 minutes, until they have risen and are firm to the touch.

4. Remove the cupcakes from the pan and cool on a cooling rack.

5. To make the frosting, in a small bowl, beat together the cream cheese, butter, confectioners' sugar, and vanilla extract until smooth. Beat in half the shredded coconut.

6. Spread the frosting smoothly over each cooled cupcake into a snowball shape. Sprinkle with the remaining coconut and serve.

CARROT CUPCAKES

Anyone who is a fan of carrot cake will absolutely adore these cupcakes. With the addition of grated orange zest, they are a moreish alternative.

MAKES 12 CUPCAKES

CUPCAKES
10 tablespoons (1¼ sticks) butter, softened
⅔ cup packed light brown sugar
3 eggs, lightly beaten
1¼ cups self-rising flour
½ teaspoon baking powder
1 teaspoon ground allspice
1 cup ground walnuts
Grated zest of 1 orange
1⅓ cups grated carrots
⅓ cup golden raisins

FROSTING
½ cup cream cheese
2¼ cups confectioners' sugar
1 tablespoon lemon juice
Chopped walnuts, to decorate

1. Preheat the oven to 350°F. Line a cupcake pan with 12 paper cupcake liners.

2. In a large bowl, beat the butter with the sugar, eggs, flour, baking powder, ground allspice, ground walnuts, and orange zest until light and creamy.

3. Stir in the grated carrots and raisins until evenly mixed. Spoon the mixture into the paper liners.

4. Bake in the preheated oven for 25 minutes until they have risen and are just firm to the touch. Let cool in the pan for 5 minutes, then transfer to a cooling rack to cool.

5. For the frosting, in a medium bowl, beat the cream cheese until smooth and creamy. Beat in the confectioners' sugar and lemon juice.

6. Spread over the tops of the cakes using a small metal spatula and scatter with chopped walnuts to decorate.

MARMALADE MADEIRA CUPCAKES

Including both orange marmalade and candied orange peel, these cupcakes are heaven on a plate for anyone who enjoys orange-flavored cakes and desserts.

MAKES 12 CUPCAKES

10 tablespoons (1¼ sticks) butter, softened
⅓ cup superfine sugar
¼ cup orange marmalade
2 eggs, lightly beaten
1⅓ cups self-rising flour
½ teaspoon baking powder
1 teaspoon vanilla extract
Piece of candied orange peel

1. Preheat the oven to 350°F. Line a cupcake pan with 12 paper cupcake liners.

2. In a large bowl, beat the butter with the sugar, marmalade, eggs, flour, baking powder, and vanilla extract until light and creamy.

3. Spoon the mixture into the paper liners. Cut thin strips from the candied orange peel and lay a couple of slices over each cupcake.

4. Bake in a preheated oven for 20 minutes until they have risen and are just firm to the touch.

5. Remove the cupcakes from the pan and cool on a cooling rack.

PLUM & "POLENTA" CUPCAKES

Instead of flour, these cupcakes are made with cornmeal, or "polenta" in Italy, and ground almonds. Topped with plums and finished with a lemon-flavored honey drizzle, these little cakes are bound to impress.

MAKES 8 CUPCAKES

3 tablespoons mild olive oil or vegetable oil, plus extra for greasing
1 cup cornmeal
½ cup superfine sugar
1 teaspoon baking powder
¾ cup ground almonds
½ teaspoon almond extract
⅓ cup sour cream
Finely grated zest of 1 lemon, plus 4 teaspoons juice
2 eggs, lightly beaten
2 fresh red plums, pitted and cut into thin wedges
2 tablespoons honey

1. Preheat the oven to 350°F. Lightly grease 8 cups in a nonstick or silicone cupcake pan with oil.

2. In a large bowl, mix together the cornmeal, sugar, baking powder, and ground almonds in a bowl.

3. In a separate bowl, beat together the almond extract, sour cream, oil, lemon zest, and eggs until combined. Add the wet ingredients to the dry ingredients and mix to form a thick paste.

4. Spoon the mixture into the prepared cups and arrange a couple of plum wedges on top of each. Bake in the preheated oven for 20–25 minutes until they have risen and are beginning to color around the edges.

5. Let cool in the pan for 5 minutes, then loosen the edges with a knife and transfer to a cooling rack.

6. Pierce the tops of the cakes with a skewer. Mix together the lemon juice and honey, and drizzle over the cakes while still warm.

CHERRY COLA COTTON CANDY CUPCAKES

It's the mountain of pink frosting on top of these cherry cola cupcakes that inspires the name of cotton candy cupcakes. Top with a shiny, fresh red cherry or "popping candy" for the maximum wow factor.

MAKES 12 CUPCAKES

CUPCAKES

1⅔ cups self-rising flour
3 tablespoons unsweetened cocoa
¼ teaspoon baking soda
⅔ cup superfine sugar
2 eggs, lightly beaten
⅔ cup cherry cola
¼ lb (1 stick) butter, melted

FROSTING

¼ lb (1 stick) butter, softened
¾ cup confectioners' sugar, sifted
Scant ½ cup heavy cream
1–2 drops of red food coloring
¼ cup boiling water
12 fresh red cherries or
   2–3 teaspoons popping candy,
   to decorate (optional)

1. Preheat the oven to 375°F. Line a cupcake pan with 12 paper cupcake liners.

2. In a large bowl, sift the flour, cocoa, and baking soda together and stir in the sugar. Make a well in the center of the dry ingredients, add the eggs and cola, and beat using an electric beater. Add the melted butter and beat until smooth.

3. Spoon the mixture into the paper liners and bake in the preheated oven for 20–25 minutes, until they are risen and firm. Transfer to a cooling rack to cool.

4. To make the frosting, beat the butter, confectioners' sugar, and heavy cream until well blended. Beat in a drop or two of food coloring until the color resembles a pale cotton-candy pink, then add boiling water a tablespoon at a time, until it all comes together as a light glossy frosting.

5. Either spoon the frosting onto the cupcakes, shaping into a peak with the back of the spoon, or put the frosting into a pastry bag and pipe it over the cupcakes to resemble cotton candy. Top each cake with a cherry or a sprinkling of popping candy, if liked, and serve immediately.

ALMOND & GINGER CUPCAKES

These sophisticated little cupcakes are wonderfully moist, but light and airy at the same time. They could easily be served plain, but they do look pretty with a thin layer of frosting and some toasted slivered almonds.

MAKES 12 CUPCAKES

CUPCAKES

1¼ cups self-rising flour

½ cup ground almonds

⅔ cup superfine sugar

⅔ cup milk

¼ lb (1 stick) butter, melted

2 eggs, lightly beaten

2–3 drops of almond extract

2 pieces preserved ginger in syrup, drained and finely chopped, plus 1 tablespoon of the drained syrup

FROSTING

⅔ cup confectioners' sugar

1 tablespoon milk

1 tablespoon toasted slivered almonds, to decorate

1. Preheat the oven to 350°F. Line a cupcake pan with 12 paper cupcake liners.

2. In a large bowl, mix the flour and ground almonds with the sugar. Add the milk, melted butter, eggs, and almond extract, and beat until smooth.

3. Stir in the ginger and syrup and spoon the mixture into the paper liners.

4. Bake in the preheated oven for about 25 minutes, until they have risen and are firm to touch. Transfer to a cooling rack to cool.

5. To make the frosting, in a small bowl, mix together the confectioners' sugar and milk until thick but runny and smooth.

6. Spoon a little frosting over each cupcake and let stand until almost set, but still sticky. Scatter with the slivered almonds and let set completely before serving.

SNOW-COVERED GINGER MUFFINS

Light, moist, and tasty, these frosting-crowned, ginger-spiced muffins are delicious with cups of steaming cappuccino or hot chocolate.

MAKES 12 MUFFINS

MUFFINS
¼ lb (1 stick) butter, plus extra for greasing (if needed)
½ cup maple syrup
½ cup packed light brown sugar
1¾ cups self-rising flour
1 teaspoon baking powder
1 teaspoon ground ginger
2 eggs, lightly beaten
½ cup milk
3 tablespoons chopped candied ginger

FROSTING
1⅔ cups confectioners' sugar, sifted
4 teaspoons water
2 pieces of glacé ginger, sliced, to decorate

1. Preheat the oven to 350°F. Line a muffin pan with 12 paper muffin liners. Alternately, grease 12 cups in a nonstick or silicone muffin pan with butter.

2. In a medium saucepan over low heat, add the butter, syrup, and sugar, and heat gently, stirring, until the butter has melted.

3. Meanwhile, in a medium bowl, mix the flour with the baking powder and ground ginger. In a separate small bowl, beat the eggs with the milk.

4. Take the saucepan off the heat and beat in the flour mixture. Gradually beat in the egg and milk mixture, then stir in the candied ginger.

5. Spoon the mixture into the paper liners and bake in the preheated oven for 10–15 minutes, until they are well risen and have cracked. Transfer to a cooling rack to cool.

6. For the frosting, sift the confectioners' sugar into a small bowl and gradually mix in the water to create a smooth, not-too-runny frosting.

7. Drizzle random lines of icing from a spoon over the muffins and decorate with slices of ginger. Allow to set completely for 30 minutes before serving.

SWEET CHAMOMILE MUFFINS

Split these chamomile-flavored muffins and serve warm with butter for the perfect snack to serve with a soothing cup of tea. For a more lively version, substitute the chamomile tea with peppermint tea and use 3½ oz chopped white chocolate instead of the golden raisins.

MAKES 12 MUFFINS

6 tablespoons lightly salted butter, melted, plus extra to serve and for greasing (if needed)
3 tablespoons chamomile tea (either loose leaf or from bags)
¾ cup ground almonds
½ cup superfine sugar
2¼ cups all-purpose flour
1 tablespoon baking powder
Finely grated zest of 1 lemon
½ cup golden raisins
2 eggs, lightly beaten
1¼ cups buttermilk

1. Preheat the oven to 425°F. Line a muffin pan with 12 paper muffin liners. Alternately, grease 12 cups in a nonstick or silicone muffin pan with butter.

2. Put the tea, ground almonds, and sugar in a food processor, and process briefly until combined. Turn into a large bowl and stir in the flour, baking powder, lemon zest, and raisins.

3. In a medium bowl, mix together the melted butter, eggs, and buttermilk, then add the mixture to the dry ingredients. Stir the ingredients together until just combined.

4. Spoon the mixture into the paper liners and bake in the preheated oven for 15–18 minutes until they have risen and are pale golden.

5. Transfer the muffins to a cooling rack to cool a little and serve warm, split and buttered.

STRAWBERRY BUTTERFLY CUPCAKES

These pretty little strawberry and vanilla cupcakes are perfect for any princess's tea party! Serve topped with a delicious wild strawberry if possible, otherwise a drizzle of homemade strawberry jelly.

MAKES 12 CUPCAKES

CUPCAKES

¼ lb (1 stick) butter, softened
½ cup superfine sugar
2 eggs, lightly beaten
1 teaspoon vanilla extract
1 cup self-rising flour
1 teaspoon baking powder
2 tablespoons milk
8 dried strawberries, finely chopped

VANILLA CREAM

½ cup mascarpone cheese
2–3 tablespoons confectioners' sugar
Seeds scraped from 1 vanilla bean
1–2 teaspoons milk, if needed
12 wild strawberries or 2 tablespoons good-quality strawberry jelly, warmed, to decorate

1. Preheat the oven to 375°F. Line a cupcake pan with 12 paper cupcake liners.

2. In a large bowl, beat the butter and sugar together until pale and creamy. Beat in the eggs and vanilla extract, a little at a time, beating well between each addition.

3. Gently fold in the flour, baking powder, milk, and dried strawberries and spoon the mixture into the paper liners.

4. Bake in the preheated oven for 20–25 minutes, until they are risen and are firm to touch. Transfer to a cooling rack to cool.

5. For the vanilla cream, in a small bowl, beat the mascarpone with the confectioners' sugar and vanilla seeds, adding a teaspoon or two of milk to loosen, if necessary.

6. Use a small, sharp knife to cut a circle of sponge from the top of each cupcake, then cut each top in half. Fill the hole with the vanilla cream and replace the tops so that they resemble butterfly wings. Top each one with either a fresh, wild strawberry or a drizzle of strawberry jelly, and serve.

LAVENDER CUPCAKES

What better way to welcome the early signs of spring than picking some fresh lavender flowers and baking these delicious cupcakes?

MAKES 12 CUPCAKES

CUPCAKES
6 lavender flowers, plus extra small sprigs to decorate
¼ lb (1 stick) butter, softened
⅔ cup superfine sugar
Finely grated zest of ½ orange
2 eggs, lightly beaten
1¼ cups self-rising flour
½ teaspoon baking powder

FROSTING
1¼ cups confectioners' sugar
4–5 teaspoons orange juice
A few drops of lilac food coloring

1. Preheat the oven to 350°F. Line a cupcake pan with 12 paper cupcake liners.

2. Pull the lavender flowers from their stems and put in a large bowl with the butter, superfine sugar, orange zest, eggs, flour, and baking powder. Beat until light and creamy.

3. Spoon the mixture into the paper liners and bake in the preheated oven for 20 minutes, until they have risen and are just firm to touch. Transfer to a cooling rack to cool.

4. For the frosting, in a small bowl, mix the confectioners' sugar with enough orange juice to make a thin glaze, then stir in the food coloring.

5. Spread the frosting over the cakes and decorate with small sprigs of lavender flowers.

PINK ROSE CUPCAKES

These rosy cupcakes topped with a creamy frosting will impress your friends.
Serve them as an afternoon treat along with a refreshing cool drink.

MAKES 12 CUPCAKES

CUPCAKES

2 sugared rose petals, plus extra
   to decorate
²/₃ cup superfine sugar
¼ lb (1 stick) butter, softened
2 eggs, lightly beaten
1¼ cups self-rising flour
½ teaspoon baking powder
1 tablespoon rose water

FROSTING

1 cup mascarpone cheese
1 cup confectioners' sugar
1 teaspoon lemon juice
A few drops of pink food coloring
   (optional)

1. Preheat the oven to 350°F. Line a cupcake pan with 12 paper cupcake liners.

2. Put the sugared rose petals and superfine sugar in a food processor, and process until the rose petals are chopped into small pieces.

3. In a large bowl, add the rose petal mixture with all the remaining cake ingredients. Beat until light and creamy.

4. Spoon the mixture into the paper liners and bake in the preheated oven for 20 minutes, or until they are risen and just firm to touch. Transfer to a cooling rack to cool.

5. For the frosting, in a medium bowl, beat together the mascarpone, confectioners' sugar, lemon juice, and food coloring, if using, until smooth.

6. Spread the frosting over the tops of the cakes using a small metal spatula and decorate with extra sugared rose petals.

BLUEBERRY CHEESECAKE CUPCAKES

These colorful cupcakes are bursting with blueberries and covered with a divine, slightly chewy, vanilla cheesecake topping.

MAKES 12 CUPCAKES

CHEESECAKE FILLING

Generous 1 cup mascarpone cheese
⅔ cup granulated sugar
Seeds scraped from 1 vanilla bean
1 egg

CUPCAKES

5 tablespoons butter, softened
⅓ cup superfine sugar
2 eggs, lightly beaten
1¼ cups all-purpose flour
1 teaspoon baking powder
Pinch of salt
2–3 tablespoons milk
⅔ cup fresh or frozen blueberries

1. Preheat the oven to 350°F. Line a cupcake pan with 12 paper cupcake liners.

2. For the cheesecake filling, in a medium bowl, beat the mascarpone with the sugar, vanilla seeds, and egg until smooth.

3. In a separate large bowl, beat together the butter and sugar until pale and creamy. Add the eggs, one at a time, beating well and adding a tablespoon of flour between each addition.

4. Sift the remaining flour with the baking powder and salt over the eggs and fold gently, adding 2–3 tablespoons milk to create a good dropping consistency.

5. Stir in the blueberries, then spoon the mixture into the paper liners, leaving a dip in the center.

6. Pour the cheesecake filling over each cupcake and bake in the preheated oven for 30–35 minutes, until they have risen and the cheesecake topping is golden.

7. Let the cupcakes cool in the pan for 2–3 minutes, then transfer to a cooling rack. Serve slightly warm or cold.

MOCHACCINO CUPCAKES

The strong cocoa taste in these dark cupcakes works wonderfully with the whipped coffee cream "froth" on top of these mochaccino cupcakes, which are sprinkled with chocolate for an authentic finish!

MAKES 12 CUPCAKES

CUPCAKES
1¼ cups self-rising flour
½ cup unsweetened cocoa
⅔ cup superfine sugar
2½ tablespoons powdered
  cappuccino mix
¼ cup boiling water
Scant ½ cup milk
¼ lb (1 stick) butter, melted
2 eggs, lightly beaten
Scant ½ cup chocolate chips

"MOCHA" TOPPING
½ cup whipping cream
1 tablespoon confectioners' sugar
1 teaspoon coffee extract
1–2 tablespoons chocolate sprinkles,
  to decorate

1. Preheat the oven to 350°F. Line a cupcake pan with 12 paper cupcake liners.

2. In a large bowl, sift the self-rising flour and cocoa together, then add the sugar.

3. In a medium bowl, dissolve the cappuccino mix in the boiling water, stir in the milk and melted butter, and beat in the eggs. Beat into the bowl of dry ingredients until smooth.

4. Fold in the chocolate chips and spoon the mixture into the paper liners. Bake in the preheated oven for 25–30 minutes, until they have risen and are springy. Transfer to a cooling rack to cool.

5. For the topping, in a large bowl, add the cream with the confectioners' sugar and coffee extract, and beat until fairly stiff.

6. Spread the topping over the cupcakes, sprinkle with the grated chocolate, and serve.

CARAMEL & CHOCOLATE CUPCAKES

MAKES 12 CUPCAKES

CUPCAKES

4 oz dark chocolate, broken into chunks
7 tablespoons butter
2 eggs, lightly beaten
⅔ cup packed light brown sugar
1 teaspoon vanilla extract
Scant ½ cup all-purpose flour
¼ cup unsweetened cocoa
Pinch of salt

CARAMEL

¼ cup packed dark brown sugar
4 tablespoons butter
3 tablespoons heavy cream
1 tablespoon dark corn syrup

1. Preheat the oven to 350°F. Line a cupcake pan with 12 paper cupcake liners.

2. In a small saucepan over low heat, slowly melt the chocolate and butter together.

3. In a large bowl, beat the eggs with the sugar and vanilla extract, then stir in the melted chocolate mixture followed by the flour, cocoa, and salt until combined.

4. Spoon the mixture into the paper liners and bake in the preheated oven for 25–30 minutes, until they have risen and are almost firm. Let the cakes cool in the pan for 5 minutes before transferring to a cooling rack.

5. Make the caramel sauce. In a small saucepan over low heat, combine the sugar, butter, cream, and corn syrup, and heat gently, stirring occasionally, until the sugar has dissolved. Simmer for 1–2 minutes, remove from the heat, and let cool to a thick pouring consistency.

6. Drizzle the sauce from side to side over the cupcakes and serve.

TIP
Why not try this mixture as mini-muffins to make some bite-size versions? Just follow the recipe, using a mini-muffin pan lined with small paper liners, and reduce the cooking time accordingly.

OTHER SMALL
BAKES

MINI CITRUS DRIZZLE LOAVES

These perfect little individual cakes are full of citrus flavors and have a wonderful moist texture, thanks to the drizzled syrup.

MAKES 6 LOAVES

LOAVES
9 tablespoons (1⅛ sticks) butter, plus extra for greasing
Finely grated zest of 1 lemon
Finely grated zest of 1 lime
1 teaspoon orange extract
1⅔ cups self-rising flour, plus extra for dusting
⅔ cup superfine sugar
2 eggs, lightly beaten
2 tablespoons milk

DRIZZLE
⅔ cup superfine sugar
Juice and grated zest of ½ lime
Juice and grated zest of ½ lemon
Juice and grated zest of 1 orange
Confectioners' sugar, to dust (optional)

1. Preheat the oven to 350°F. Grease and lightly flour 6 mini loaf pans. Each one should measure no less than 3¾ x 2 inches.

2. In a small saucepan over low heat, melt the butter with the lemon zest, lime zest, and orange extract. Set aside to cool.

3. In a large bowl, mix the flour and sugar together, then pour in the melted butter along with the eggs and milk. Fold well until the mixture is smooth and there are no pockets of flour left.

4. Spoon the mixture into the loaf pans and bake in the preheated oven for about 25 minutes, until risen and golden.

5. Meanwhile, make the syrup. In a small saucepan over low heat, heat the sugar with the lemon and orange juice and zest until the sugar dissolves, then set aside to cool.

6. Let the loaves cool in the pans for 5 minutes before pricking all over with the tines of a fork. Slowly drizzle the syrup over the surface of the loaves and let stand until absorbed.

7. Once the syrup has soaked in, remove the cakes from their pans, dust with confectioners' sugar, if liked, and serve.

RAVANIE

There are many versions of these diamond-shaped orange cakes from Greece. Ravanie are traditionally made with flour and semolina, and this version has sesame seeds, adding a slightly crunchy texture.

MAKES 8–10 PIECES

SPONGE

¼ lb (1 stick) butter, softened, plus
   extra for greasing
1¼ cups superfine sugar
1½ cups all-purpose flour
2 teaspoons baking powder
Pinch of salt
½ teaspoon ground allspice
¼ cup fine semolina
Finely grated zest and juice of
   2 oranges
2 eggs
1 tablespoon sesame seeds, plus
   2 tablespoons, lightly toasted,
   to decorate

SYRUP GLAZE

⅔ cup superfine sugar
Finely grated zest and juice of
   1 orange
2 tablespoons honey

1. Preheat the oven to 350°F. Grease a 11 x 7-inch baking pan and line with parchment paper.

2. In a large bowl, beat the butter and sugar together until pale and creamy. In a separate bowl, sift together the flour, baking powder, salt, and allspice. Add the dry ingredients to the creamed mixture, along with the semolina, orange zest, orange juice, eggs, and sesame seeds. Mix until well combined.

3. Spread the mixture evenly in the prepared pan and bake in the preheated oven for about 1¼ hours, until firm and an inserted skewer comes out clean.

4. Meanwhile, make the syrup glaze. In a small saucepan over low heat, gently heat the sugar, orange zest, and orange juice, stirring, until the sugar has dissolved. Add the honey and boil gently for 3 minutes.

5. Pierce the cake at evenly spaced intervals with a fine skewer, then spoon the syrup glaze evenly over the top, sprinkle with the toasted sesame seeds, and let cool. Turn out of the pan and peel away the parchment paper. Cut into diamond shapes and serve.

CHOCOLATE PRETZELS

MAKES 40 PRETZELS

PRETZELS

1 tablespoon melted butter or
sunflower oil, plus extra for
greasing

1¾ cups white bread flour, plus
extra for dusting

1 teaspoon active dry yeast

2 teaspoons superfine sugar

Large pinch of salt

Scant ½ cup lukewarm water

3 oz each dark, white, and milk
chocolates, broken into chunks

GLAZE

2 tablespoons water

½ teaspoon salt

1. Lightly grease 2 large baking sheets. In a large bowl, mix the flour with the yeast, sugar, and salt. Add the melted butter or oil and gradually mix in the lukewarm water until you have a smooth dough. On a lightly floured surface, knead the dough for 5 minutes until smooth and elastic.

2. Cut the dough into quarters, then cut each quarter into 10 smaller pieces. Shape each piece into a thin rope about 8 inches long. Bend the rope so that it forms a wide arc, then bring one of the ends around in a loop and secure about halfway along the rope. Do the same with the other end, looping it across the first secured end.

3. Transfer the pretzels to the greased baking sheets. Cover loosely with lightly oiled plastic wrap and let stand in a warm place for 30 minutes, until they are well risen.

4. Meanwhile, preheat the oven to 400°F. In a small bowl, make the glaze by mixing the water and salt until the salt has dissolved, then brush this over the pretzels.

5. Bake the pretzels in the preheated oven for 6–8 minutes, until golden brown. Transfer to a cooling rack and let cool.

6. In a heatproof bowl set over a saucepan of barely simmering water, melt the dark chocolate. Using a spoon, drizzle random lines of chocolate over the pretzels. Let harden, then repeat the process with the white chocolate, using a clean heatproof bowl, and then the milk chocolate.

7. When the milk chocolate has set, store in an airtight container and eat within 2 days.

CARDAMOM COFFEE FRIANDS

Very popular in Australia, friands come in all kinds of different flavors.
These delicious little muffin-like cakes have been spiked with cardamom
coffee, giving them a sophisticated, must-try taste.

MAKES 12 FRIANDS

12 tablespoons (1½ sticks) butter,
   melted and cooled, plus extra
   for greasing
¼ cup strong espresso coffee
1⅔ cups confectioners' sugar, plus
   extra for dusting
6 cardamom pods, crushed lightly
1⅓ cups ground almonds
⅔ cup all-purpose flour
5 egg whites

1. Preheat the oven to 375°F. Grease a 12-hole friand or small muffin pan with melted butter.

2. To make the cardamom coffee syrup, in a small, heavy saucepan over low-medium heat, add the strong espresso and stir in ⅓ cup of the confectioners' sugar and the crushed cardamom pods. Bring to a boil and simmer for 2–3 minutes to create a light syrup. Set aside to cool.

3. In a large bowl, add the ground almonds and sift in the flour and remaining confectioners' sugar.

4. In a separate medium bowl, lightly beat the eggs whites until frothy, then gently fold them into the bowl with the ground almonds. Lightly fold in the melted butter and 2–3 tablespoons of cardamom coffee syrup until just combined.

5. Spoon the mixture into the prepared pan and bake in the preheated oven for about 20 minutes, until pale golden and firm.

6. Cool the friands in the pan for 2–3 minutes before turning out onto a cooling rack. Serve while still slightly warm with a sprinkling of confectioners' sugar, or cool completely and store in an airtight container.

CHOCOLATE-ORANGE MADELEINES

MAKES 24 MADELEINES

¾ cup superfine sugar

3 eggs

½ teaspoon orange extract

Pinch of salt

1½ cups all-purpose flour, plus extra
for dusting

½ teaspoon baking powder

Finely grated zest of 1 orange

¼ lb (1 stick) butter, melted, plus
extra for greasing

1–2 tablespoons freshly squeezed
orange juice

Vegetable oil, for greasing

10½ oz orange-flavored dark
chocolate, broken into chunks

1. In a large bowl, beat together the sugar, eggs, orange extract, and salt for 4–5 minutes, or until doubled in volume. Fold in the flour, baking powder, and orange zest, then add the butter and the orange juice. Cover and place in the refrigerator for at least 2 hours, or preferably overnight.

2. Preheat the oven to 425°F. Grease 24 madeleine molds with melted butter, then dust lightly with flour, tapping out any excess. Remove the mixture from the refridgerator, stir gently, and fill each mold about three-quarters full.

3. Bake in the preheated oven for 4 minutes, then reduce the oven temperature to 350°F and bake for 4–5 minutes more, until risen and firm and golden. Immediately remove the madelaines from the pan and transfer to a cooling rack to cool.

4. Wash and dry the madeleine molds, then grease lightly with some paper towel dipped in vegetable oil.

5. In a heatproof bowl set over a pan of barely simmering water, melt the chocolate. Fill each mold with about 2 teaspoons of the melted chocolate, using the back of the spoon to ensure the mold is well covered.

6. Gently push each cooled madeleine back into a mold and let stand in a cool place for the chocolate to set completely. Use the tip of a knife to gently lever a chocolate-shelled madeleine out of its mold—once set it should come out easily.

LAVENDER-HONEYED MADELEINES

These pretty little cakes have a delicate perfumed taste from the use of dried lavender flowers. Try substituting the honey for your favorite flavor, such as ginger or elderflower, and replacing the flowers with freshly grated ginger root or dried elderflowers.

MAKES 18 MADELEINES

½ cup sugar

2 eggs

2 tablespoons lavender honey

Pinch of salt

¾ cup all-purpose flour, sifted,
   plus extra for dusting

½ teaspoon baking powder

1–2 teaspoons dried sweet
   lavender flowers

5 tablespoons butter, melted,
   plus extra for greasing

Fresh lavender flowers,
   to decorate

1. In a large bowl, beat together the sugar, eggs, honey, and salt for 4–5 minutes, or until doubled in volume. Fold in the flour, baking powder, and lavender flowers, then add the butter. Cover and place in the refrigerator for at least 2 hours, or preferably, overnight.

2. Preheat the oven to 425°F. Grease 18 madeleine molds with melted butter, then dust lightly with sifted flour, tapping out any excess.

3. Remove the mixture from the refrigerator, stir gently, and fill each mold about three-quarters full.

4. Bake in the preheated oven for 4 minutes, then reduce the oven temperature to 350°F and continue baking for 4–5 minutes more, until risen and golden. Immediately remove the madeleines from the molds and cool on a cooling rack.

5. Serve decorated with lavender flowers. These are best served the day they are made.

TIP
Use an unsprayed "sweet" variety of lavender. The amount you use depends on how strong you want the perfumed taste of lavender to be.

FRENCH MADELEINES

You will need shell-shaped madeleine molds for these little cakes.
They are just the right size for small sponges that are crispy at
the edges and soft and airy in the middle.

MAKES 18–20 MADELEINES

¼ lb (1 stick) butter, melted, plus
   extra for greasing
3 eggs
⅔ cup superfine sugar
Finely grated zest of 1 lemon
1 cup self-rising flour, plus extra
   for dusting
½ teaspoon baking powder
Confectioners' sugar, for dusting

1. Preheat the oven to 425°F. Grease the molds of 2 madeleine pans with melted butter, then dust lightly with flour, tapping out any excess.

2. In a large bowl, beat together the eggs, sugar, and lemon zest until thick and pale and the whisk leaves a thin trail when lifted from the bowl.

3. Sift the flour and baking powder into the bowl and gently fold in. Drizzle the melted butter around the edges of the mixture and fold in until just combined.

4. Spoon the mixture into the prepared molds, making each about two-thirds full. Bake in the preheated oven for 10–12 minutes until risen and deep golden.

5. Let the cakes cool in the pan for 5 minutes, then ease them out of the molds with a metal spatula and cool on a cooling rack. Serve dusted with confectioners' sugar.

MADELEINES AU CITRON

These light lemony French cakes are delicious served as an afternoon snack. Chill the mixture well before baking to ensure the bulging peaks form in the center of the cakes.

MAKES 12 MADELEINES

⅓ cup superfine sugar

2 medium eggs

Finely grated zest of 1 lemon

Pinch of salt

⅔ cup all-purpose flour, plus extra
    for dusting

½ teaspoon baking powder

4 tablespoons butter, melted,
    plus extra for greasing

1 tablespoon milk

1. In a large bowl, beat together the sugar, eggs, lemon zest, and salt for 4–5 minutes until thick and doubled in volume. Fold in the flour and baking powder, then add the butter and milk. Cover and place in the refrigerator for at least 2 hours, or preferably overnight.

2. Preheat the oven to 425°F. Grease 12 madeleine molds with melted butter, then dust lightly with flour, tapping out any excess.

3. Remove the mixture from the refrigerator, stir gently, and fill each mold about three-quarters full.

4. Bake in the preheated oven for 4 minutes, then reduce the temperature to 350°F and cook for 4–5 minutes more until risen and golden.

5. Immediately remove the madeleines from the molds and transfer to a cooling rack to cool. These are best served the day they are made.

ORANGE PALMIERS WITH PLUMS

These crisp, delicate pastries look professional, but they can be made in minutes using store-bought puff pastry. Simply unravel, sprinkle with sugar and grated orange zest, roll up, and slice. Sandwich baked pastries with a warm plum compote or vary the fruit to suit the season—rhubarb and raspberries also work well.

SERVES 4

Vegetable oil, for greasing
1 frozen puff pastry sheet, about
   10 inches square, thawed
Beaten egg, for brushing
3 tablespoons light brown sugar
Finely grated zest of ½ orange
Generous ⅓ cup orange juice
¼ cup superfine sugar
2½ cups pitted and sliced plums
Confectioners' sugar, sifted,
   to dust
Crème fraîche, or equal quantities
   of sour cream and whipping cream
   mixed together, to serve

1. Preheat the oven to 400°F and lightly grease a baking sheet.

2. Brush the pastry with beaten egg, then sprinkle with the brown sugar and orange zest. Roll one edge of the pastry until it reaches the middle. Do the same from the opposite edge until both rolls meet.

3. Brush the pastry with more beaten egg, then cut into 8 thick slices. Arrange the pastry slices, cut side uppermost, on the prepared baking sheet and bake in the preheated oven for 10 minutes until they are well risen and golden.

4. Meanwhile, in a medium saucepan over low-medium heat, add the orange juice, sugar, and plums, and cook, uncovered, for 5 minutes.

5. Sandwich the palmiers in pairs with the plums, dust with sifted confectioners' sugar, and serve with crème fraîche.

MILK CHOCOLATE CHIP FRIANDS

Friands are typically made in oval-shaped molds, but if you don't have one, just use small, preferably silicone, muffin molds.

MAKES 12 FRIANDS

7 tablespoons butter, melted, plus extra for greasing
4 egg whites
Generous 1 cup ground almonds
⅓ cup ground hazelnuts
Scant ½ cup all-purpose flour
1¼ cups confectioners' sugar
Pinch of salt
Generous ½ cup milk chocolate chips

1. Preheat the oven to 400°F. Lightly grease a 12-hole friand or small muffin pan with melted butter.

2. In a large bowl, beat the egg whites to break them up, being careful not to overbeat them; they should be frothy and foamy, but not stiff.

3. Add the ground almonds and hazelnuts to the eggs, and sift in the flour with the sugar and salt. Fold in gently until just combined. Carefully fold in the melted butter along with the chocolate chips.

4. Spoon the mixture into the prepared molds and bake in the preheated oven for about 12 minutes, until they have risen and are golden.

5. Remove the friands from the molds and cool on a cooling rack.

BAKLAVA-STYLE TARTLETS

MAKES 12 TARTLETS

PASTRY SHELLS

¼ lb (1 stick) butter, melted, plus
  extra for greasing
5 phyllo pastry sheets, 12 x 16 inches

SYRUP

¼ cup water
⅓ cup granulated sugar
1 tablespoon honey
2 teaspoons lemon juice
1 teaspoon orange flower water

NUT FILLING

Scant ½ cup shelled pistachios
Scant ½ cup walnut pieces
¼ teaspoon ground cinnamon
Generous pinch of ground cloves

1. Preheat the oven to 350°F. Grease 12 cups in a nonstick or silicone cupcake pan with melted butter.

2. To make the syrup, in a small, heavy saucepan over low heat, add the water, sugar, honey, and lemon juice, and heat until the sugar has dissolved. Simmer gently for about 5 minutes, then remove from the heat and stir in the orange flower water. Set aside.

3. Place the pistachios and walnuts in the small bowl of a food processor and process until finely chopped, but not ground. Turn into a bowl and stir in the ground cinnamon and cloves.

4. Cut the pile of phyllo pastry sheets into 4-inch squares. This should give you 12 piles, each with 5 layers of pastry.

5. Take one pile of pastry layers and brush both sides of each sheet with melted butter. Lay one on top of the other, turning each one slightly so that the pastry has a pretty, starred edge. Lay this pile in a prepared cupcake cup and push down to line it. Repeat this process with the remaining piles of pastry, then spoon the nut filling into each one.

6. Bring the pastry corners in toward the center of each nut filling, almost encasing the nuts so that they look like little parcels. Drizzle any remaining butter over the tops of the tartlets.

7. Bake in the preheated oven for about 20 minutes, until crisp and golden. Leaving the tartlets in the pan, spoon over the reserved syrup. Let stand to cool to allow the syrup soak in before serving.

ALMOND MACAROONS

With no extra ingredients added to the basic recipe, this is a delicious traditional macaroon. If you like the taste of marzipan, then you will love their flavor.

MAKES 16 MACAROONS

1⅓ cups ground almonds
¾ cup superfine sugar
2 large egg whites
½ teaspoon almond extract

1. Preheat the oven to 350°F. Line 3 baking sheets with parchment paper.

2. In a medium bowl, mix the ground almonds and superfine sugar until well combined.

3. In a large bowl, beat the egg whites with the almond extract until stiff and glossy. Add the ground almond mixture to the egg whites and gently fold in until evenly blended.

4. Using a small teaspoon, place spoonfuls of the mixture on the baking sheets, leaving space between them so that they can expand slightly. Bake in the preheated oven for 15 minutes, until golden and slightly firm.

5. Remove the macaroons from the oven and let cool for 5 minutes. When set, lift them off the parchment paper with a thin metal spatula and cool completely on a cooling rack. Store in an airtight container.

CHOCOLATE MACAROONS

Crispy on the outside and moist on the inside, little chocolate macaroons make a stylish accompaniment to coffee after Christmas dinner.

MAKES 25 MACAROONS

2 egg whites
½ cup superfine sugar
1⅓ cups ground almonds
½ cup grated dark chocolate
25 chocolate-covered coffee beans,
   to decorate

1. Preheat the oven to 375°F. Line a large baking sheet with parchment paper.

2. In a large bowl, beat the egg whites until stiff, then gradually whisk in the sugar until the mixture is thick and glossy. Gently fold in the ground almonds and grated chocolate.

3. Put the mixture into a large pastry bag fitted with a large plain tip and pipe small rounds, about 1½ inches in diameter, onto the baking sheet. Alternatively, place small teaspoons of mixture on the baking sheet.

4. Press a chocolate-covered coffee bean into the center of each macaroon. Bake in the preheated oven for about 15 minutes, until they have slightly risen and are just firm.

5. Remove the macaroons from the oven and cool for 5 minutes. When set, lift them off the parchment paper with a thin metal spatula and cool completely on a cooling rack.

TIP
Chocolate-covered coffee beans are available from some supermarkets and coffee specialists. If you can't find them, decorate each macaroon with a whole blanched almond.

PINK LAMINGTONS

MAKES 24 LAMINGTONS

SPONGE

Butter, for greasing

5 eggs

Generous ¾ cup superfine sugar

1 cup self-rising flour

Scant ½ cup cornstarch

1 cup shredded, dried coconut

TOPPING

2 cups shredded, dried coconut

4 cups confectioners' sugar

⅓ cup hot water

⅓ cup warm milk

Few drops of red food coloring

TIP

Use other food coloring, if liked. Green for Saint Patrick's Day; red, white, and blue for Independence Day; or a deep, red for Christmas.

1. Preheat the oven to 350°F. Grease a deep 13 x 9-inch baking pan and line the bottom with parchment paper.

2. In a large bowl, beat the eggs with an electric beater for about 5 minutes until thick, frothy, and tripled in volume. Add the sugar a tablespoon at a time, beating constantly until the mixture is pale, glossy, and leaves a trail. This will take another 5 minutes.

3. Sift the flour and cornstarch into the egg mixture, then fold in gently with the dried coconut until just combined. Turn the mixture into the pan and bake in the preheated oven for 25–30 minutes until it has risen and is springy. An inserted skewer should come out clean.

4. Turn the cake out onto a wire rack and let cool. Once cool, peel away the parchment paper and cover with a clean, dry dish towel. Let stand in a cool place for several hours, preferably overnight.

5. Cut the sponge cake into 24 squares. For the topping, turn the coconut evenly onto a large, flat plate. In a bowl, beat the sugar, hot water, and warm milk together, and place the bowl over a saucepan of hot water.

6. Using two forks, one at a time, lift 12 of the sponge squares into the sugar mixture to coat. Let the excess mixture drip off, then roll the square in the coconut to cover. Place on a cooling rack to set.

7. Add 1–2 drops of red food coloring to the runny confectioners' sugar mix, stirring well and adding more to turn a deep, vivid pink color, if liked. Finish coating the remaining 12 squares of sponge in the same way.

QUICK HAZELNUT MELTS

These hazelnut cookies are quick to prepare—you can even use the food processor to beat the butter and sugar together—and they may be just as quick to disappear, as they literally melt in your mouth.

MAKES 20 COOKIES

¼ lb (1 stick) butter, softened, plus
   extra for greasing
⅓ cup blanched hazelnuts
¼ cup superfine sugar
1¼ cups all-purpose flour

1. Preheat the oven to 375°F and grease a baking sheet.

2. Grind the hazelnuts in a food processor until smooth but still retaining a little texture.

3. In a heavy skillet over low heat, brown the nuts until evenly golden. Pour them into a small bowl and stir until cool.

4. In a large bowl, beat the butter with the sugar until pale and creamy. Add the flour and cooled nuts, and beat again to make a soft dough.

5. Take walnut-size pieces of dough and shape into balls, then pat into flat ovals. Place on the prepared baking sheet and flatten slightly with a fork.

6. Bake in the preheated oven for 12 minutes, until just golden, then let cool on a cooling rack. Store in an airtight container.

STRAWBERRIES & CREAM TARTLETS

MAKES 12 TARTLETS

PASTRY DOUGH

1 cup all-purpose flour, plus extra
for dusting

4 tablespoons cold butter

2 tablespoons confectioners' sugar

Seeds scraped from ½ vanilla bean

1 egg yolk

2–3 tablespoons cold water

FILLING

½ cup mascarpone cheese

Scant ½ cup heavy cream

2 tablespoons seed-specked vanilla
sugar

9 oz fresh strawberries, washed,
hulled, and sliced

1. Place the flour and cold butter in the bowl of a food processor and process until the mixture resembles fine bread crumbs.

2. Add the confectioners' sugar and vanilla seeds, pulse quickly, and then add the egg yolk and just enough cold water to bind the pastry. Wrap in plastic wrap and place in the refrigerator for about 30 minutes.

3. Preheat the oven to 350°F. Lightly grease 12 cups in a nonstick or silicone cupcake pan. Cut out 12 parchment paper disks, about 4 inches in diameter. You will also need some pie weights or dried beans.

4. Roll out the pastry thinly on a lightly floured surface and use a 3½-inch round cutter to cut out 12 circles of pastry, gently pressing each one into a cupcake cup.

5. Place a circle of parchment paper over each pastry, fill with a few pie weights, and bake in the oven for about 10 minutes. Remove the weights and the paper, and return to the oven for 7–10 minutes more, until the pastry shells are crisp and golden. Remove from the pan and let cool on a cooling rack.

6. In a medium bowl, beat together the mascarpone, heavy cream, and vanilla sugar until thick and unctuous. Spoon into the cold pastry shells, top with the sliced strawberries, and serve immediately.

SPICED CHOCOLATE PASTRIES

Oozing with molten chocolate, these unusual pastry triangles are delicious with either a cup of tea or freshly brewed coffee.

MAKES 9 PASTRIES

Butter, for greasing
8 oz puff pastry, thawed if frozen
Flour, for dusting
1 egg yolk
2 tablespoons milk
18 squares of dark chocolate
1 teaspoon grated orange zest
Pinch of ground star anise

1. Preheat the oven to 400°F and grease a baking sheet.

2. Roll out the pastry thinly on a lightly floured surface and trim to form a 9-inch square. Cut into thirds crosswise and lengthwise to form 9 squares.

3. In a small bowl, beat the egg yolk and milk together to make a glaze. Brush a little around the edges of each pastry square.

4. Place 2 squares of chocolate, a little orange zest, and a touch of star anise on each pastry square. Fold diagonally in half and press the edges together to seal.

5. Place the pastries on the prepared baking sheet and bake in the preheated oven for 12 minutes, until they have risen and are golden.

6. Let the pastries cool on a cooling rack for a few minutes before serving.

CHOCOLATE & BANANA SAMOSAS

These sweet samosas are filled with a winning combination—banana and chocolate—and are delicious hot, straight from the oven. Serve with lightly whipped cream or ice cream.

MAKES 12 SAMOSAS

2 ripe bananas, coarsely mashed
½ cup dark chocolate chips
12 phyllo pastry sheets, each about
    12 x 7 inches
Melted butter, for brushing
Confectioners' sugar, for dusting

1. Preheat the oven to 350°F. Line a baking sheet with parchment paper.

2. In a medium bowl, mix the bananas with the chocolate chips. Set aside.

3. Fold each sheet of phyllo pastry in half lengthwise. Place a large spoonful of the banana mixture at one end of the phyllo strip and then fold the corner of the phyllo over the mixture, covering it in a triangular shape. Continue folding the pastry over along the length of the strip of pastry to make a neat triangular samosa.

4. Moisten the edge with water to seal and place on the prepared baking sheet. Repeat with the remaining filling and pastry.

5. Brush the samosas with melted butter and bake in the preheated oven for 12–15 minutes, or until lightly golden and crispy. Remove from the parchment paper, dust with confectioners' sugar, and serve hot.

TIP
When working with phyllo pastry, always keep the pastry covered with a damp dish towel to prevent it from drying out, until ready to use.

CONVERSION CHARTS

To help you enjoy these recipes wherever you live, here is a list of key easy-to-follow conversions that have been rounded up or down. To ensure the best results, never mix your measures—choose either imperial and cups or metric—and stay with that system. Cup measures are based on the American imperial measuring cup. One American cup holds 8 fl oz, 16 tablespoons, or 240 ml.

OVEN TEMPERATURE

°Farenheit	°Celcius	Gas mark
225°F	110°C	¼
250°F	120°C	½
275°F	135°C	2
300°F	150°C	2
325°F	160°C	3
350°F	180°C	4
375°F	190°C	5
400°F	200°C	6
425°F	220°C	7
450°F	230°C	8

LIQUID CONVERSIONS

American	Imperial	Metric
1 teaspoon	1 teaspoon	5 ml
1 tablepoon	½ fl oz	15 ml
2 tablepoons	1 fl oz	30 ml
¼ cup	2 fl oz	60 ml
⅓ cup	2¾ fl oz	85 ml
½ cup	4 fl oz	120 ml
¾ cup	6 fl oz	180 ml
1 cup	8 fl oz	240 ml
1¼ cups	½ pint	300 ml
2½ cups	1 pint	600 ml
3 cups	1¼ pints	750 ml
4 cups	1¾ pints	1 liter

WEIGHTS

Imperial	Metric
¼ oz	10 g
½ oz	15 g
¾ oz	20 g
1 oz	25 g
4 oz	115 g
4½ oz	125 g
6 oz	175 g
7 oz	200 g
8 oz	225 g
12 oz	340 g
1 lb	450 g
1½ lb	675 g
2¼ lb	1 kg

DIMENSIONS

Imperial	Metric
1 inch	2.5 cm
2 inches	5 cm
3¼ inches	8 cm
3½ inches	9 cm
4 inches	10 cm
5 inches	12.5 cm
7 inches	18 cm
8 inches	20 cm
9 inches	23 cm
10 inches	25.5 cm
11 inches	27.5 cm
12 inches	30 cm
13½ inches	34 cm

US CUP CONVERSIONS

1 US Cup	Metric
almonds, ground	95 g
almonds, slivered	110 g
berries, fresh	150 g
cheese, soft, such as cream cheese, mascarpone	220 g
cocoa, unsweetened	110 g
coconut, dried, shredded	95 g
coconut, fresh, grated	80 g
cornflakes	25 g
cornmeal	150 g
cornstarch	125 g
dried fruits, such as currants, raisins, sultanas	145 g
dried fruit, chopped, such as dates, apricots	175 g
dried fruit, cranberries	145 g
flour, all-purpose/self-rising	150 g
flour, rice	160 g
flour, wholewheat	125 g
honey	225 g
jelly, jam, marmalade	320 g
muesli with fruit and nuts	85 g
nuts, chopped	115 g
nuts, whole	145 g
oats, rolled	100 g
peanut butter, chunky	260 g
pine nuts	115 g
semolina	175 g
sugar, caster/granulated	200 g
sugar, confectioners'	140 g
sugar, packed brown	220 g
walnuts, chopped	125 g

BUTTER CONVERSIONS

Imperial	Metric
1 tablespoon	15 g
2 tablespoons (¼ stick)	25 g
3 tablespoons	40 g
4 tablespoons (½ stick)	60 g
5 tablespoons	75 g
6 tablespoons (¾ stick)	85 g
7 tablespoons	100 g
8 tablespoons (¼ pound, 1 stick)	115 g
9 tablespoons	125 g
10 tablespoons	140 g
12 tablespoons	170 g
14 tablespoons (1¾ sticks)	200 g
1 cup (½ pound, 2 sticks)	225 g
18 tablespoons	250 g
2 cups (1 pound, 4 sticks)	450 g

GLOSSARY

US term	British term
allspice	mixed spice
almonds, slivered	almonds, flaked
applesauce	apple purée
beets	beetroot
cherries, candied	cherries, glacé
chocolate, dark	chocolate, plain
coconut, shredded	coconut, desiccated
cornmeal	polenta
cornstarch	cornflour
cotton candy	candyfloss
crackers, graham	biscuits, digestive
cream, heavy	cream, double
cutting board	chopping board
flour, self-rising	flour, self-raising
flour, all-purpose	flour, plain
ginger, preserved	ginger, stem
liners, paper	cases, paper
mixer, electric	hand whisk, electric
pan, jelly roll	pan, Swiss roll
paper, parchment	paper, baking
paper, wax	paper, greaseproof
pastry shell	pastry case

US term	British term
pastry, phyllo	pastry, filo
pie weights	baking beans
pitted	stoned
oil, canola	oil, rapeseed
raisins, golden	sultanas
saucepan, heavy	saucepan, heavy-based
skillet	frying pan
soda, baking	soda, bicarbonate of
sugar, brown	sugar, soft brown
sugar, confectioners'	sugar, icing
sugar, raw brown	sugar, demerara
sugar, superfine	sugar, caster
syrup, corn	golden syrup
toffee, sponge	honeycomb
toothpick	cocktail stick
towel, dish	towel, tea
vanilla bean	vanilla pod
wholewheat	wholemeal
wrap, plastic	clingfilm
yeast, active dry	yeast, fast-action dried
yogurt, plain	yoghurt, natural
zucchini	courgette

INDEX